# FLYING TO THE SUN

## A HISTORY OF BRITAIN'S HOLIDAY AIRLINES

CHARLES WOODLEY

The History Press

Cover illustrations: front: top, Four Eagle Aviation Vikings, 1950s. (Via Peter Brown); bottom, Skyways of London, 1950s. (Via author); rear, L–R: early BKS inclusive tour passengers disembark from a Dakota, Costa Brava; Aquila Airways luggage label. (Via Dave Thaxter); 1939 Thomas Cook Air Travel brochure (Thomas Cook).

First published 2016

The History Press
The Mill, Brimscombe Port
Stroud, Gloucestershire, GL5 2QG
www.thehistorypress.co.uk

© Charles Woodley, 2016

The right of Charles Woodley to be identified as the Author of this work has been asserted in accordance with the Copyright, Designs and Patents Act 1988.

British Library Cataloguing in Publication Data.
A catalogue record for this book is available from the British Library.

ISBN 978 0 7509 5660 4

Typesetting and origination by The History Press
Printed and bound in Malta by Melita Press

# CONTENTS

# ACKNOWLEDGEMENTS

Many people have assisted me in the preparation of this book, providing images and permission to reproduce historical data, anecdotes or simply encouragement. These include: Dave Thaxter, Andrew Reid, Nick Savage, John Camm, Clare Hunt at the Southend Museums Service, Ralf Mantufel, Klaus Vomhof, Dietrich Eggert, Dick Gilbert, Hazel at the Monarch Airlines Press Office, Peter Brown, members of the Homage to Court Line online forum, Claire Borgeat at the Thomson Press Office, Graham M. Simons, Amy Rigg and all the team at The History Press, and my wife Hazel.

I have made efforts to identify and credit the owners of all images used, but to anyone I may have overlooked I offer my sincere apologies and thanks.

# INTRODUCTION

The return of peace after the Second World War saw the war-weary population of Britain craving for a way to exchange their austere surroundings for a sunlit beach in a new country, if only for a week or two.

The cessation of hostilities resulted in the demobilisation of large numbers of RAF aircrew and engineers and the disposal of hundreds of war surplus transport aircraft at knockdown prices. The combination of these factors led to the formation of many charter airlines in the late 1940s and the first inclusive tour packages to destinations such as the south of France. These were only for the well-heeled, but in 1949 Vladimir Raitz began offering holidays by air to tented accommodation in Corsica, and the public responded with enthusiasm.

Holiday destinations such as Majorca and Benidorm grew from little more than fishing villages, and the UK charter airlines also benefitted from the operation of holiday charter flights out of West Berlin, an activity denied to German airlines by a post-war ban.

Many new UK operators sprang up in the 1950s, but most of these had insufficient financial resources to survive beyond their first one or two summer seasons. A particularly bad year for the charter industry was 1961, when the collapse of several of its contracted airlines (with the resultant knock-on bad publicity) led the prominent tour operator Universal Sky Tours to set up its own in-house airline, Euravia (later to be renamed Britannia Airways).

Even a financial tie-up with a major tour company was no guarantee of security for a holiday airline, and in 1974 Court Line Aviation was brought down by the collapse of the Clarksons Holidays Group. Those operators who did survive showed great resourcefulness in finding ways to circumvent the government restrictions imposed on them. 'Flight-only' arrangements, which included 'throwaway' vouchers for rudimentary accommodation in hostels or even tents, found a ready market, and entrepreneur Freddie Laker eventually secured approval to undercut the scheduled service fares to North America with his Skytrain no-reservations flights.

In more recent times, large sums of money have been invested in fleets of brand new aircraft as state of the art as those of the national carriers, and a new market for long-haul holidays has been exploited.

Within Europe, the role of the charter airlines has today largely been displaced by the activities of low-cost carriers such as easyJet and Ryanair, but I hope this book will serve as a reminder of days past and a fitting tribute to those entrepreneurs who brought about a travel revolution.

Charles Woodley
Aberdeenshire

# 1

# Britain's Holiday Airline Industry: A Historical Overview

In 1938 legislation was introduced entitling workers in the UK to one week's paid holiday each year, but at that time overseas travel was still beyond the means of all but the 'leisured classes', and the outbreak of the Second World War in 1939 put thoughts of travel for pleasure on hold for the next five or six years.

The return of peace in 1945 saw the return to Britain of thousands of service personnel who had been sent to continental Europe and Asia, and who were keen to experience more of the world and escape for a while from the rationing and drabness of post-war Britain.

The rundown of the RAF in the aftermath of the ending of hostilities released into civilian life a large number of aircrew and aircraft engineers who hoped to continue in aviation as a living. Many of these saw an opportunity to set up their own charter airlines using some of the hundreds of war surplus transport aircraft that were being disposed of at knockdown prices to carry holidaymakers to the sunshine and beaches of the south of France, Italy and Spain.

To do this, they needed to establish a working relationship with a travel agent who could arrange the necessary accommodation and sell the package to the public. One of the first to see the potential for overseas holidays by air was Vladimir Raitz. In 1949 he was a 27-year-old, working for the Reuters news agency when he was invited by a friend to take a vacation at his friend's Club Olympique, a tented holiday village on a beach at Calvi in Corsica. At the end of his stay, Mr Raitz was offered the chance, with some colleagues, to purchase a concession on a large area of beach nearby, and he seized on the idea of operating holidays to it by air.

At that time Calvi possessed an airstrip built by US forces during the Second World War, but it had no airport buildings and there was no direct air service to it from the UK. On his way back from Calvi, Mr Raitz made a detour to take a look at the Spanish island of Majorca, which also had an airfield and was served by flights from Barcelona. Although impressed by the tourist potential of the island, he decided to concentrate his initial efforts on providing holidays to Corsica.

On arrival back in London he made enquiries about chartering an aircraft for a series of flights to Calvi. He was quoted a price of £305 per round trip for a thirty-two-seat Dakota aircraft, but was also warned that he was unlikely to be granted the necessary government approval for the flights as the state airline British European Airways held a monopoly on all British air services to Europe. The fact that they did not operate to anywhere near Calvi was irrelevant. Undeterred, he set up a holiday company called Horizon Holidays, using money left to him by his grandmother.

In March 1950 he was informed by the Ministry of Civil Aviation that approval had been granted for the charter flights, but only for the carriage of students and teachers – a restriction that was to be dropped in later years. Horizon Holidays hastily produced its first holiday 'brochure' (in reality a four-page leaflet), offering tours to Calvi for a package price of £32 10s 0d, flying from the UK and staying in tented accommodation with meals and wine included. Great emphasis was placed on the plentiful quantities of food on offer, as Britain was still in the grip of meat rationing at that time.

In due course, tours to Majorca followed, bringing the first summer tourism to an island which had achieved a degree of fame as the winter retreat of Chopin and George Sand, and had relied primarily on winter tourism until 1951. The airfield at Son Bonet was expanded to cope with the additional traffic and, in May 1953, the UK state airline British European Airways inaugurated twice-weekly scheduled services from London, using twenty-seven-seat Vickers Vikings flying out of the RAF base at Northolt while Heathrow was under reconstruction. A refuelling stop at Bordeaux was necessary, and the fare was £39 3s 0d return.

Elsewhere in Spain, today's major resorts were yet to be discovered by foreigners. In 1950 Benidorm was a small coastal fishing village with a grand total of 102 hotel rooms. The newly appointed mayor, Pedro Zaragoza Orts, had noted the growth of tourism in northern Europe. Recognising the tourist potential of his location, he set about developing the facilities. He arranged for running water to be piped to the village from 10 miles away, and then contacted all the major European scheduled airlines. As a result, tourists began to arrive in increasing numbers.

One problem that arose concerned beachwear. The bikini was banned in staunchly Catholic Spain, but from 1953 Mayor Zaragoza permitted it to be worn on the beaches of Benidorm. The backlash was immediate and drastic. The Civil Guard escorted bikini wearers off the beaches, and the mayor was threatened with excommunication from the Catholic Church. Undaunted, he travelled by motor scooter all the way to Madrid to see the ruler, General Franco, and was accorded his backing.

Tourist travel to Spain was still in its infancy in the early 1950s, and British citizens still had to obtain an expensive visa to enter the country. A 1952 newspaper survey

→ A 1949 advertisement for BEA's inclusive air holidays. (Via author)

← A view of the Benidorm beach scene around 1964. (Via author)

→ The beach area at Benidorm around 1965. (Via author)

revealed that only half of the UK population took any kind of holiday, and of these only 3 per cent travelled abroad.

In 1954 the runway at Palma's Son Bonet Airport was extended and a parallel taxiway and parking apron were added to cope with the growing number of tourists arriving by air. However, by 1956, landing on the 4,920ft-long (1,500m) runway was still a job for expert pilots as the approach was made through mountains, and a stone wall and some orange trees rendered the first 650ft (200m) of it unusable.

From 1 January 1954 the Sir Henry Lunn travel agency chain had been offering credit facilities in connection with its continental holiday programme, but between 1955 and 1960 the increase in UK average weekly earnings (including overtime) far outstripped the rise in retail prices. There was now the possibility of developing winter holiday programmes to areas such as Tunisia, Algeria and Morocco, and of offering affordable holidays to Madeira and the Canary Islands, which until then had only been the playgrounds of the wealthy.

During the summer of 1957, British European Airways (BEA) obtained about 14 per cent of its revenue from the 'inclusive tour fares' available to travel agents using its scheduled service flights to create holiday packages. In the financial year 1955–56 the independent airlines had earned some £365,000 from the operation of inclusive tour charter flights, but this was a small proportion of their total revenues of around £17 million. By far their biggest money earner (£6.725 million) was the operation of trooping flights to British Army bases in the Middle East and Singapore. This was about to change, however, as the overseas military presence was run down and holiday charters expanded, and not only from UK airports.

Since the end of the Second World War there had been a ban on German airlines operating services out of West Berlin. All scheduled and charter services were reserved for aircraft of the 'occupying powers' (the USA, Great Britain and France), and the UK independent airlines secured lucrative contracts from major German tour operators for charter flights to the Mediterranean resorts. This work was to expand and continue well into the era of wide-bodied jets.

Majorca's original airport at Son Bonet was no longer able to cope with the increased volume of traffic and was unable to be extended, so in 1958 Spain's National Airport Plan proposed the construction of a new large commercial airport at Son Sant Joan to serve the island. This was opened on 7 July 1960, and during that year around 150,000 passengers were carried into and out of Palma by UK scheduled and charter airlines.

The growth of the charter airlines attracted scrutiny from shipping lines anxious to diversify into air transport now that their traditional market was being eroded by scheduled air travel. Many of them acquired substantial financial interests in the independent carriers during the 1950s and early 1960s. During 1960, 2.25 million Britons holidayed abroad and in the summer of 1961 UK holidaymakers comprised the majority of visitors to Majorca, but even so most of the population still stayed loyal to resorts such as Blackpool instead of venturing abroad.

The year 1961 was a black one for the charter airlines, with the demise of Overseas Aviation, Air Safaris, Falcon Airways and Pegasus Airlines, all based at Gatwick and nearly all undercapitalised and thus ill-equipped to deal with the slump in traffic during the winter months. By the summer of 1962 the remaining companies were also having to compete with foreign charter airlines such as Italy's SAM and the Spanish carrier Aviaco, both of which were the charter subsidiaries of their countries' state airlines.

In the mid-1960s travelling abroad by air was still something of a novelty to a lot of people in Britain, and, unlike today, many holidaymakers wore their Sunday best for the flights. From 1963 the Biggin Hill Air Fair was held at the famous Battle of Britain airfield in Kent each May, and a variety of charter airlines made aircraft such as the Douglas DC-6B, Caravelle and BAC One-Eleven available there for the public to queue up to inspect inside and out. There were even short pleasure flights in such typical holiday charter airliners, all geared to overcoming any doubts about holidaying overseas by air.

One of the most popular revenue earners for the tour operators and independent airlines at this time was the operation of day trips by air to the Dutch tulip fields from airports around the UK. Most of these were organised by the newly established Clarksons Tours, whose meteoric growth and dramatic collapse would later shake the travel industry. In April 1966 a day trip from Bristol to the tulip fields cost £9, and included flights to Rotterdam and back in a Dakota aircraft of Dan-Air Services and coach travel from there to Keukenhof, with brief stops at Delft and The Hague.

By 1969 the renamed Clarksons Holidays Ltd had become Europe's largest low-cost inclusive tour operator, and had sparked off a price war by offering fourteen nights' full-board accommodation in Majorca and flights from the UK for £50, and taking an allocation of some 6,000 of the 10,000 or so hotel beds available in Benidorm.

It was around this time that Clarksons, in conjunction with local agent Gold Case Travel, and the *Newcastle Evening Gazette*, organised a 'Holiday Spectacular' on a mid-January evening at Teesside Airport. They expected around 2,000 people to attend, but in the event over 15,000 queued patiently to look around the interiors of a Dan-Air Comet 4 and BAC One-Eleven on the tarmac.

The public's appetite for overseas travel was no longer confined to Europe and the Mediterranean. At the end of 1965 the first ever programme of charter packages to the USA was unveiled, featuring flights by Caledonian Airways. By 1971, however, the UK was heading into a recession which was exacerbated by high unemployment and industrial action. This included a postal strike which played havoc with the processing of travel documents and payments.

Britain's support of Israel during the Arab–Israeli War of 1973 led to an Arab embargo on oil from the Arab states that slashed the UK's supplies by 40 per cent. Fuel prices soared, and tour operators were forced to impose fuel surcharges on the published price of holidays. Industrial action by miners caused the declaration of a State of Emergency on 13 November 1973, under which a three-day working week was imposed in order to preserve coal stocks used to generate electricity.

In 1974 airlines using UK airports were restricted to an allocated amount of fuel each month. When the Italian charter airline SAM used up its entire January allocation in three weeks its request for additional supplies was refused. In retaliation the Italian Government banned charter flights to Italy by British carriers. One of the first to feel the effect of this was Dan-Air at Gatwick, where around 100 passengers waiting to board were told that their flight had been cancelled.

As a result of all this chaos, bookings for overseas holidays slumped by 30–40 per cent, and many tour operators and charter airlines went out of business. Further problems were faced by passengers on holiday charter flights in the mid-1970s, as a series of industrial disputes involving Spanish air traffic control staff led to closures of Spanish airspace for up to seventy-two hours at a time, and in 1974 Clarksons Holidays and its airline, Court Line Aviation, suddenly ceased operations. Some sources later estimated that in the five years leading up to the collapse some 8 million holidays had been on offer at an average of £1 below cost price.

By 1975 many UK residents had acquired timeshare apartment accommodation in Mediterranean resorts and so they did not need to buy holiday packages that included a hotel stay. However, the regulations required the inclusion of accommodation in tour prices. To get around this rule, the tour operator Cosmos introduced 'cheapies' holidays to Greece for £59, the price including charter flights and a throwaway voucher for very basic hostel-type accommodation, often in shared rooms without hot and cold running water. In the years to come 'seat-only' sales would become big business for the tour operators, and by 1988 around 20 per cent of charter flight passengers would be travelling on this basis.

In the late 1980s another price war erupted as the major tour operators hired more and more aircraft and flooded the market with holidays. In the ensuing battle for market share, price discounting became the norm. During 1987 and 1988 four new charter airlines began serving the inclusive tour market, despite there already being more than a dozen established carriers. In 1989 the top thirty British tour operators made a collective loss, leading to cutbacks in their flight programmes.

From 1990, however, the situation improved, and by 1993 the overall inclusive tour market had increased by 10 per cent, with over 13 million passengers being carried that year. In an effort to improve their year-round utilisation and tap into new markets, many of the independent airlines diversified into scheduled service operations, but this proved a costly exercise and the collapse of major carriers such as Dan-Air Services and Air Europe caused the others to rethink and curbed any further expansion in this direction.

By the summer of 1994 UK charter airlines were carrying 40 per cent of the EU total, with the most popular route still being London–Palma. For the summer of 1998 a dozen or so UK airlines were operating more than 150 aircraft, representing some 36,000 seats. The daily utilisation of each aircraft averaged over twelve flying hours, and this productivity, coupled with some of the lowest employee costs in Europe, made British charter airlines the envy of their continental European rivals.

By 1998 the continued growth in scheduled services by British Airways and its franchisees made it virtually impossible for the holiday charter airlines to obtain additional landing slots at the major UK airports at sociable hours. The only way they could carry more passengers was to introduce larger aircraft onto existing services. The following years were to see the introduction of types such as the Airbus A300 and the Boeing 757, which could not only carry more passengers to the main Mediterranean resorts but could also be used on long-haul routes to North America and the Far East.

During the year 2000 the largest UK charter airlines, in terms of passengers/kilometres flown were: Britannia Airways (21,747 million), Airtours International (18,750 million), Air 2000 (17,950 million), JMC Airlines (14,300 million) and Monarch Airways (13,650 million). All of these carriers were subsidiaries of, or had alliances with, major tour operators.

# 2

# THE RELEVANT LEGISLATION

Since the early post-war years the activities of Britain's holiday airlines and their tour operator partners have been regulated by various pieces of government legislation, the earlier examples of which were introduced to safeguard the interests of the state-owned British European Airways (BEA). In later more liberal years, legislation was used to protect the interests of the consumer in the wake of the financial collapse of several major tour operators and independent airlines.

The Civil Aviation Act of 1946 reserved all air services within the UK, and from the UK to Europe, with the exception of one-off ad hoc charter flights, for BEA. If an independent airline wanted to operate a regular series of flights to a destination it had to do so under a BEA Associate Agreement, which BEA would only grant if it considered the route to be one which posed no threat to its own scheduled services, even if these did not operate to the proposed destination or anywhere in the vicinity.

However, there were loopholes to be exploited. The Act only applied to single-destination routes, so the independent airlines could operate 'aerial tours' to two or more points without an Associate Agreement. Thus, tour operators could devise and sell two-centre tours which combined such destinations as Majorca and the Costa Brava. The Act also did not encompass tours organised for members of closed groups and sold to them via organisations such as the Royal Automobile Club.

One of the first tour operators to develop this market was Whitehall Travel, set up to offer holidays to British Civil Service staff and their families. Its founder, George Wenger, explained in its first brochure:

Whitehall Travel has been formed by a group of Civil Service staff associations with the aim of providing holidays abroad at the lowest possible cost to their members. By keeping the overheads to a minimum, by private charter of aircraft, and by fullest use of bulk facilities it has been possible to offer members better value for their money than they could obtain through any commercial agency. The only means of reducing the cost of air travel is by chartering complete aircraft, but the Civil Aviation Act forbids members of the general public from taking advantage of such facilities. The various organisations of the National Staff side of the Civil Service are considered closed societies for the purposes of the Act, and permission has consequently been received to make private arrangements with one of the best known charter companies. The terms agreed upon are extremely favourable.

Another major user of this loophole in 1959 was Milbanke Tours. The Air Transport Advisory Council (ATAC) had refused them permission for a series of inclusive tours to Palma, Perpignan and Nice, using aircraft of Hunting-Clan Air Transport. Milbanke Tours advised their potential customers that if they all joined the International English Language Association they could still book their holidays, as Milbanke was the official booking agent for that organisation and they would then be members of a closed group. An irate Ministry tried to bring a prosecution, but this was thrown out by Feltham magistrates and the tours were permitted to go ahead.

The ATAC was set up in 1947 to consider licence applications from the independent airlines. Under its terms of reference it was intended:

> … to reduce the cost of air transport to the taxpayer and to give greater opportunities for private enterprise to take part in air transport developments, without in any way impairing the competitive strength of the Corporations' international air services.

In practical terms, at that time no independent airline was permitted to operate 'regular' air services (as opposed to one-off, ad hoc charter flights) except under a BEA Associate Agreement. These were only granted for routes which BEA considered too unprofitable to operate with its own aircraft.

In 1952 the newly elected Conservative government laid down new terms of reference for the ATAC, under which it was to consider applications from the independent airlines for the operation of programmes of inclusive tour charter flights, provided that such air services did not 'materially divert' traffic from the state airlines, and to consider applications for 'the operation on any route of vehicle ferry services, which could also carry a limited number of incidental passengers'. A BEA Associate Agreement would still be needed for journeys that amounted to 'a systematic service operated in such a manner that the benefits thereof are available to members of the public'.

Travel agencies, and the charter airlines they used, soon learned to make their flights 'non-systematic' and/or only available to closed groups, thus avoiding the need to apply for Associate Agreements. One of the pioneers of such tour programmes was Horizon Holidays, which initially only carried parties of students, nurses and teachers.

In its annual report for 1954–55 the ATAC observed that:

The general outcome of the hearings and the recommendations of the Council was that a much greater number of inclusive tour services were approved by the Minister than in previous years. The Council are convinced that the traffic which will for the most part be carried on these services will not be traffic which BEA would ordinarily carry, or which would in other circumstances travel by air at all. They consider that these services should be of value in stimulating the interests of new sections of the public in air transport and that they may therefore in the long run prove to be of indirect benefit to the Airways Corporations. For the most part, inclusive tour services were recommended for operation in 1955 only, although this was not intended in any way to prevent companies from submitting fresh applications for similar services in later years. It may prove possible, when further information is available from traffic figures for the summer of 1955 about their effects on the normal scheduled services of established operators, to approve inclusive tour services for slightly longer periods than hitherto.

In 1956 the ATAC dealt with 428 applications.
  In its 1956–57 annual report BEA said:

We informed the ATAC in 1955 that we would not oppose applications from the independent operators for inclusive tour services at weekends during the summer months. The volume of these services to the main Continental holiday centres has, however, now grown far beyond the scale which could be regarded as economically helpful in dealing with peak traffic demands. The size of the problem is reflected by the proportion of the total summer traffic between the United Kingdom and the Continent carried by independent operators on inclusive tour services. In the summer of 1956 they carried 27% of the total air traffic to Spain, 15% to Switzerland, 17% to northern Italy, 18% to France (excluding Paris), and 21% to Munich and Austria. In our view these operations have caused material diversion of the traffic from BEA's services.

In its 1958–59 annual report, BEA said, 'We cannot afford to be excluded from the cheap holiday market', and complained of the diversionary effect of inclusive tour flights operated by the independent airlines. BEA said it was 'imperative' that the corporation should recover its position in this 'most rapidly growing sector of European air travel'. Accordingly, they urged through the International Air Transport Association, a measure whereby they could cut fares on scheduled services to the prime holiday resorts, so that they could offer reductions of up to

25 per cent for the summer of 1959 to travel agents using their services as part of their package tours.

## THE UK TRAVEL ALLOWANCE

Concerned about the possible loss to the Exchequer of sterling being converted to foreign currencies and spent overseas by holidaymakers, the UK Government has traditionally limited the amount that can be used in this way. The personal allowance has fluctuated over the years since the end of the Second World War, from £100 in early 1951 to £50 in the autumn of that year, then to £25 in January 1952, up to £40 in the 1953 Budget and gradually upwards again until it was increased to £100 in October 1954.

A sterling crisis in July 1966 led to a reduction to £50 in the form of traveller's cheques, plus £15 in cash (intended for use only when the traveller returned to the UK). On 18 November 1967 the government was forced to devalue the pound by more than 14 per cent. Among other things, this led to the introduction of the so-called V Form. Tour operators had to declare on this the cost of the overseas ground elements paid for in foreign currency, and this amount was deducted from the traveller's £50 allowance. In the early 1970s the foreign travel allowance was increased to £300.

## AIR TRANSPORT LICENSING BOARD

In 1959 the Ministry of Aviation was created as part of the break-up of the Ministry of Supply. The 1949 Civil Aviation Act was repealed, and in 1960 the Civil Aviation (Licensing) Act was introduced. The Air Transport Advisory Council was abolished, and in its place came the Air Transport Licensing Board (ATLB). It had a brief which included ensuring easier access to routes and licences for the independent airlines.

In 1960 UK airlines needed to apply to the Director of Aviation Safety for an Air Operator's Certificate (AOC) before they could carry fare-paying passengers, and they also had to apply to the ATLB for a B Licence for inclusive tour charter flights. The application was made in conjunction with the relevant tour operator or travel agent, and covered a regular series of flights for the exclusive carriage of passengers on a specified holiday. The licence usually had provisions regarding the cost of the holiday, and licences were issued after having considered the fitness of the tour operator (in particular, the financial fitness).

The ATLB also looked into the operator's insurance arrangements, and even the conditions of service of its employees. The first large batch of inclusive tour licences was issued at the beginning of 1962, but the board usually rejected far more applications than it granted.

However, as tourism to France, Italy and Spain boomed, these countries and others formed their own charter airlines. The ATLB was hard pressed to refuse them traffic rights, as it knew that the governments of these carriers would probably take retaliatory action against British airlines. If a tour operator had its joint application with a UK charter airline turned down, it would then contract its flights out to a foreign carrier, knowing that this application would then be approved. During 1962 the foreign airlines' share of the UK inclusive tour market increased by one-third.

## PROVISION ONE

Until 1968 the minimum package holiday price was not allowed to undercut the scheduled service fare charged by BEA for the route in question. This piece of legislation was known as Provision One, and was there to protect the revenue of the state airline, although there were certain exceptions for flights to the more distant European destinations.

For 1969, however, the government permitted the tour operators to set their prices at the 1968 levels, effectively allowing a decrease in prices in real terms. Again in 1971, the minimum summer tour prices were allowed to be pegged at summer 1970 levels, but by then the pressure for a change in the legislation had subsided somewhat anyway, as the independent airlines had begun to fear that lower overall tour prices would lead to demands from tour operators for lower charter rates at a time of overcapacity in the charter market.

In 1971 the government announced that the Provision One minimum price restriction would be lifted for the winter of 1971–72 on holidays of seven nights or less, and in October 1972 Provision One was abolished completely.

## INCLUSIVE TOUR EXCURSION (ITX) FARES

In the 1960s, in order to be able to compete with charter flights on their leisure routes, ITX fares were offered by the scheduled airlines belonging to the International Air Transport Association (IATA). These could only be used by IATA-appointed travel agents and tour operators to construct package holidays using scheduled flights. The fares for individual travellers were roughly 75 per cent of the public excursion fare, dropping to around 65 per cent for groups of fifteen or more using night flights.

## AFFINITY GROUP CHARTER FLIGHTS

In 1953 IATA adopted a resolution permitting its member airlines to negotiate cut-price charter rates:

> … with one person on behalf of a group whose principal aims, purposes and objectives are other than air travel and where the group has sufficient affinity existing prior to the application for charter transportation to distinguish it and set it apart from the general public.

The agent could not take more than 5 per cent commission; membership of the so-called 'affinity group' must not exceed 20,000, and anyone flying on one of its charter flights must have been a member for six months or more. The affinity group rule was originally created to allow the non-IATA wholly owned charter subsidiaries of state airlines to operate low-cost group charters to the USA.

In Britain, the intended beneficiaries were BEA Airtours and BOAC Charters, but from 1964 onwards a large number of UK independent airlines used the affinity group loophole to obtain permits to operate transatlantic charter flights. Although some of the groups that were carried qualified under the rules, the overwhelming majority of them were invented purely to fill charter flights. The regulations specified three months' advance booking as well as six months' prior membership, but many of the 'specialist' travel agencies that sprang up to service this market issued bogus backdated membership cards, sometimes done on the day of departure.

By spring 1971, more and more passengers were being stopped and interrogated by Department of Trade inspectors at their departure airport. Many passengers who could not satisfy the inspectors were denied boarding, and the airline they were to have used was also fined. There were reports at the time of the inspectors being tipped off by rival airlines.

## ADVANCE BOOKING CHARTERS

In October 1972 the UK Civil Aviation Authority announced its plans for introducing advance booking charter flights onto North Atlantic routes. The UK airlines were invited to apply for the appropriate licences immediately, in order to be in a position to begin operating the flights from 1 April 1973.

Student charter flights and the largely discredited affinity group charter flights were to be phased out by the end of September 1973, but a category of 'common interest' or 'special event' charter flights would be retained in order to cater for events such as football supporters' charter flights. Advance booking charter flights required an advance booking period of ninety days (later reduced to four weeks, then two weeks). A minimum group size of fifty passengers was specified, but any number of different groups could be carried on the same aircraft. Only round-trip bookings of at least fourteen days' duration were permitted. Refunds were allowed, and up to 10 per cent of the names on the passenger list could be substituted up to thirty days before the departure date.

When applications for licences opened in 1972 one of the first to be received was from Jetsave, with a proposed fare of £49 return to New York. The world's first advance booking charter flight was operated on 2 April 1973 from Manchester to Toronto, with 250 passengers travelling on a newly acquired Douglas DC-10 of Laker Airways. At that time Freddie Laker was still battling to gain government approval for his proposed Skytrain walk-on transatlantic service. With the introduction of Skytrain in the late 1970s, and the introduction of low fares by the competing IATA airlines in response, advance booking charters ceased to be viable by the mid-1980s.

## THE AIR TRAVEL ORGANISER'S LICENCE

The Civil Aviation Authority was established under the Civil Aviation Act 1971, and the Air Travel Organiser's Licence (ATOL) was introduced to provide financial protection for holidaymakers. The licence came into effect in 1973, and all travel organisers (but not airlines) whose primary mode of transportation was by air must hold an ATOL. They must obtain a bond to be used to provide refunds to passengers affected by any event which causes an airline to be unable to provide booked air travel, and to cover the cost of repatriation flights and accommodation for those stranded abroad.

Following the collapse of the Court Line Group in 1974, which revealed insufficient bonding cover to provide refunds for holidays paid for but not taken, the government introduced the Air Travel Reserve Fund Act 1975, under which a levy (initially 1 per cent) was added to the price of all bookings to cover any shortfall in the amount of the operator's bond in the event of a collapse. This was launched with a £15 million loan from public funds, to be repaid from the levy.

# 3

# UK Holiday Charter Airports

During the early days of the development of the inclusive tour industry, charter flights were operated from many of Britain's regional airports and also from airports serving London and the south-east of England. Since then, many of these airports have changed out of all recognition. Some have been greatly developed, and some no longer serve the same purpose, although they continue in use as airfields in some form.

## BLACKBUSHE AIRPORT

Blackbushe Airport is situated some 34 miles south-west of London on the A30. Today it is a busy flight training and air taxi centre, but from November 1942 it was known as RAF Hartford Bridge. During the Second World War it was used by Spitfires and Mustangs, as well as light bombers.

In autumn 1943 the FIDO (Fog Investigation and Dispersal Operation, or 'Fog, Intensive Dispersal Of') was installed to aid landings in fog. Pipes were laid along each side of the runway, through which fuel was pumped and lit at perforated points to form a flare path.

In the early hours of 6 June 1944, Boston aircraft of the RAF took off from the airfield to lay smoke off the Normandy beaches on one of the first air missions of D-Day and on 19 December 1944 the airfield was renamed Blackbushe after a nearby farm. In June 1945 work started on a new passenger terminal building to handle RAF transport flights, and post-war this was used by many military VIPs.

Blackbushe closed as an RAF station on 15 November 1946, and on 1 January 1947 it was taken over by the Ministry of Civil Aviation (MCA) for use by the independent airlines. The terminal building was converted for civil use, and by July 1947 four companies were based there, one of the first being Silver City Airways which used Avro Lancastrians (converted Lancaster bombers) for charter flights to long-haul destinations such as Johannesburg. At first, customs facilities were only available by prior booking, but in 1948 these became permanent.

Many charter companies established engineering bases at Blackbushe, but one of the problems was that part of the airfield was on the other side of the A30 main road, which had to be controlled by traffic signals when aircraft were towed across to the maintenance area.

On 29 November 1948 the first and only use of the FIDO system took place when a Vickers Viking of Airwork Ltd took off to carry an urgently needed consignment of currency to West Africa.

During the 1950s the airport was much used in September of each year by military aircraft bringing VIP visitors to the air show at nearby Farnborough. In October 1950 Air Transport Charter moved in and began operating some of the first inclusive tour flights out of Blackbushe, to Corsica, Jersey and Guernsey during the following summer, and when Airwork Ltd began using four-engined Hermes aircraft on trooping flights in 1952 the terminal building was expanded, with a new two-storey building being linked to the existing facility by a covered corridor.

Eagle Airways commenced a scheduled passenger service in June 1953 from Blackbushe to Belgrade with Vickers Vikings, and in January 1955 they were joined by Dan-Air Services. In October 1956 the US Navy moved its FASRON 200 air transport unit across from Hendon and by 1959 many independent airlines had established bases at Blackbushe with the state airlines, BEA and BOAC, also using the airport for crew training flights by aircraft as large as the Bristol Britannia and the Comet 4.

The MCA's requisition of the airfield was due to expire at the end of 1960, and for various reasons its successor, the Ministry of Transport and Civil Aviation, decided not to acquire the land. To allow time for clearance of the site, the earlier date of 31 May 1960 was set for the closure of flying operations. Most of the airlines moved to the newly opened Gatwick Airport, but Blackbushe was to reopen for light aircraft operations in September 1962.

## MANSTON AIRPORT

Manston Airport, in Kent, was first used as a flying site by the Royal Flying Corps in 1917. During the interwar years the airfield was expanded, and from early 1940 it was used as an emergency diversion airfield for RAF bombers. To this end, a special very long emergency runway was added in 1944, and the FIDO fog landing system was added later. After the end of the Second World War Manston was designated as an 'RAF and Civil Customs Aerodrome'.

The Cold War years saw it being used by aircraft of the United States Air Force as USAF Manston between December 1956 and June 1958. It then reverted to being a joint RAF/civil airfield, and in April 1958 former Wing Commander H.C. Kennard of Silver City Airways opened the first airline service, using Hermes airliners to

Le Touquet in France as part of the 'Silver Arrow' coach-air service from London to Paris. He later resigned from Silver City and set up his own airline, Air Ferry, also based at Manston.

In 1963 Air Ferry's Vickers Viking and Douglas DC-4 aircraft arrived to operate inclusive tour flights, and on 30 March 1963 one of the DC-4s inaugurated the airline's first passenger service from Manston. After Air Ferry was taken over by the Air Holdings Group, Wing Commander Kennard resigned and started up Invicta Airways, also based at Manston, which operated its first revenue service from Manston on 20 March 1965.

Manston was also used for cargo charter flights by Invicta and other airlines, and after the demise of Invicta it saw sporadic inclusive tour use by airlines such as Dan-Air Services and Aviogenex. In 1989 the airport was rebranded as Kent International Airport, and a new terminal building was opened.

## LUTON AIRPORT

In 1935 Luton Corporation purchased a 329.5-acre site, to be used as a flying field, for £100 per acre with the aid of a government loan. A twelve-member airport committee was formed in February 1936, and in September of that year Percival Aircraft Ltd signed a ninety-nine-year lease on a 10-acre plot to be used for aircraft manufacture. The aerodrome was officially opened on 16 July 1938 with an air pageant which included RAF aerobatics teams and a parachute jump.

During the Second World War Luton was used for aero engine testing by D. Napier & Sons, and for the manufacture of Percival Proctor aircraft, as well as Airspeed Oxfords and De Havilland Mosquitos under subcontract. Post-war, Hunting Air Travel set up a base there, and other early users included Eagle Aviation with a fleet of Avro Yorks.

In September 1950 the airport committee took the decision to build a new control tower on the north side to replace the existing wooden structure, and in 1951 the airport was granted customs facilities on a one-year trial basis. The new control tower was opened in September 1952 and in the same month the helicopter operator Autair established a base at Luton. In later years this company was to expand into fixed-wing scheduled and inclusive tour services from the airport.

On 21 December 1959 a new concrete runway, 5,432ft long by 150ft wide, became operational. Around this time work began on a new hangar with a 200ft clear span for Luton Corporation. Customs facilities were reinstated on a permanent basis, eliminating the need for international flights to make a stop en route for clearance.

The new charter airline, Euravia (eventually to become Britannia Airways), agreed to use Luton as its base in 1962, subject to improvements in the passenger amenities. These included an extension to the terminal building and in the mid-1960s work began on a new terminal building, to have three times the capacity of its predecessor. The work also included a new approach road and parking space for 450 cars, and the total cost exceeded £700,000.

By 1969 one fifth of all holiday charter flights from the UK departed from Luton, and by 1972 it had become Britain's most profitable airport. In 1973 two marquee areas had to be erected to relieve passenger congestion at peak periods. Partly because of this, in 1974 some airlines began transferring services to other airports such as Gatwick.

In November 1999 a new £40 million terminal building was opened by Her Majesty the Queen.

## SOUTHEND AIRPORT

The first recorded flight from a site at Southend took place in 1915, and flying operations continued during the First World War. On 18 September 1935 an airport at Rochford was officially opened, seeing service during the Second World War.

Southend Corporation was granted a licence to operate the airport on 31 December 1946, and during 1947 East Anglian Flying Services (later to be renamed Channel Airways) moved into Southend, and Air Charter Ltd was set up there by Freddie Laker.

In 1948 customs facilities were established, and services to the Channel Islands and Ostend were inaugurated by East Anglian Flying Services. A new terminal building was constructed during 1951, and in 1953 Dan-Air Services was formed with its first operating base at Southend. That same year BKS Aerocharter inaugurated inclusive tour flights from Southend to Calvi in Corsica.

Later, on 14 April 1955, Air Charter Ltd began 'Channel Air Bridge' car ferry services from Southend with Bristol 170 aircraft, initially to Calais, and then to Ostend from October 1955. In November 1957 another new airline, Tradair, was set up at Southend to operate inclusive tour flights. This company was later to be bought out by Channel Airways and the operations of this airline, and the car ferry services of Air Charter, transformed Southend for many years into one of Britain's busiest airports during the summer months.

On 24 December 1958 fog closed most of the London area airports and Southend accepted fifty-six diverted flights, including Viscount, Constellation and Convair aircraft, until it ran out of apron parking space.

With the failure of Channel Airways and the closure of the car ferry services, the airport languished in the doldrums for many years, but in 2008 the airport, now rebranded as London Southend Airport, was acquired by the Stobart Group and has since acquired a new control tower, railway station and terminal building. The low-cost carrier easyJet commenced services from the airport in 2012.

# GATWICK AIRPORT

In 1930 two young men who had met while learning to fly at Croydon Airport purchased a plot of land near to Gatwick Racecourse for use as a flying field. In August 1930 the airfield was issued with its first aerodrome licence, for an initial six-month period and on a very restricted basis. By 1934 a company called Airports Ltd had been set up to run airfields at Gatwick and also at Gravesend in Kent. Plans were drawn up for a new terminal building of the latest design at Gatwick, and on 6 June 1936 the official opening of the terminal and its associated hangars and parking apron took place.

During the Second World War, Gatwick was used by army co-operation aircraft such as Lysanders and Mustangs, and for aircraft servicing, but in August 1946 the airfield was derequisitioned. Its fate was uncertain for a time, but the government was persuaded to allow its use as a base for charter airlines and air taxi companies. In 1952 it was announced that Gatwick had been selected for development as London's second airport.

Plans were developed for a new terminal building and a concrete runway on a site adjacent to the existing aerodrome, and on 31 March 1956 the airfield was closed to all air traffic except the helicopters of BEA's experimental unit to allow construction work to proceed. The new Gatwick Airport, which was officially opened by Her Majesty the Queen on 9 June 1958, featured the first terminal building to combine access to air, mainline rail and trunk road facilities under one roof. The airport also had a new control tower and a new 7,000ft runway.

The first airline to establish a maintenance base at Gatwick was Transair. Other early operators included African Air Safaris and Air Links, and when Blackbushe was closed to airline traffic in 1960 many of its airlines transferred across. Another major boost to traffic that year was the formation of British United Airways and its decision to use Gatwick as its operating base.

On 1 April 1966 the airport was taken over by the new British Airports Authority. During 1967–68 a five-storey office block was constructed above the terminal building. The runway was extended to 9,075ft in length in 1970, and in 1973 to 10,165ft.

In 1983 the North Pier was replaced by a satellite terminal capable of handling eight wide-bodied airliners, and in 1985 work began on a new taxiway running parallel to the runway, which could also be used as an alternative runway in an emergency. A £200 million North Terminal, linked to the South Terminal by a driverless 'rapid transit system', was opened in 1988 by Her Majesty the Queen.

Gatwick has been used for the launching of many well-known airlines, including British Caledonian Airways, Laker Airways and Virgin Atlantic Airways.

# PIONEERING DAYS

## AIR KRUISE LTD

One of the first UK charter airlines to work in conjunction with a travel agency to offer holidays by air in the period following the Second World War was Air Kruise Ltd, which had been founded in 1946 by Wing Commander Hugh Kennard and his wife, Audrey.

The company initially used light aircraft for pleasure flying from Ramsgate and from Lympne Airfield in Kent, but during the summer of 1946 Air Kruise and Fourways Travel operated sixteen day holidays to first-class hotels on the French Riviera for £75 all in. The price included air travel from Croydon Airport to Nice in six- to eight-seat Percival Q6 aircraft, and as the flights were not operated under a BEA Associate Agreement they were, strictly speaking, illegal, but the companies do not appear to have been prosecuted.

## AIR TRANSPORT CHARTER

Another pioneering independent airline was Air Transport Charter, which was formed in July 1946 as a charter operator based in Jersey. On 2 April 1947, Air Transport Charter took delivery of its first Dakota aircraft.

In 1949 the expanded fleet of Dakotas was transferred to Blackbushe Airport in Hampshire, and during that year the company applied successfully for a BEA Associate Agreement to operate a fifteen-week summer season of flights from Newcastle to Jersey in conjunction with T.A. Bulmer & Co. A 90 per cent load factor was achieved on the Dakotas used, and in May 1950 the airline commenced a series of twenty flights between Blackbushe and Calvi on Corsica for Horizon Holidays. The Dakotas typically cruised at 170mph and an altitude of 3,000ft, and after a refuelling stop at Lyons the aircraft would arrive at Calvi some six hours or so after leaving Blackbushe.

Percival Q 6

Fourways Travel cordially invite your enquiries. When completing the enclosed booking form will you please state the resort at which you wish to spend your holiday.

**YOUR HOLIDAY
ON THE RIVIERA**

**BY AIR TO THE RIVIERA . . . . 16 DAYS, £75 INCLUSIVE**

JUAN-LES-PINS

**NICE**
HOTEL D'ANGLETERRE

or

**MONTE CARLO**
HOTEL METROPOLE

or

**JUAN-LES-PINS**
LES AMBASSADEURS

MONTE CARLO

MONTE CARLO

Passengers on this delightful tour leave London by air every Saturday, and within four to four and a half hours are basking in the sun and warmth of the French Riviera. A new, revitalized Riviera where all the pre-war luxuries may be indulged in ; dancing, swimming, sport and, of course, the fun of the famous casinos of the one and only Riviera.

These tours include the following :

1. Return passage by fast and safe twenty-one seater Percival Q.6 airliners London-London.

2. Full pension at any of the above first-class hotels, inclusive of service and taxes.

3. Transfer from the airport of arrival to the hotel and vice versa. Passengers living within a ten mile radius of Croydon will have the added luxury of being picked up at their residence by private car and conveyed to the airport of departure. On the return journey they will again be met by private car and driven to their home.

4. 44 lbs. of baggage is allowed each passenger (free of charge) on the aircraft.

Passports, visas, foreign exchange, insurance (baggage and personal) may be arranged through us at the usual rates.

Booking form is enclosed, upon receipt of which, together with a deposit of £20 per person, all necessary arrangements will be made.

**FOURWAYS TRAVEL LTD
MARSHALL & SNELGROVE**
OXFORD STREET, LONDON, W.1
MAYfair 6600 and MAYfair 4937

← A 1946 advertisement for the Fourways Travel inclusive tour programme to the south of France. (Via author)

↓ A BKS Aerocharter Dakota takes off from the rudimentary airstrip at Calvi, Corsica, in 1954, on one of the pioneering inclusive tour services. (Captain Arthur Whitlock)

↑ Two Dakotas and a Vickers Viking of BKS Air Transport and their crews at Luqa, Malta, on a charter service in 1956. (Captain Arthur Whitlock)

→ Dakota G-AJBH of Air Transport Charter at Blackbushe Airport in the 1950s.(Via Peter Brown)

→ A Dakota of Giros Aviation. (Via Peter Brown)

→ Dan-Air Dakota G-AMSS outside the terminal building at Blackbushe Airport in the 1950s. (Via Peter Brown)

Over 600 passengers were transported that season, and the flights were repeated for the summers of 1951 and 1952. Weekend services were operated to the Channel Islands, and during the winter parties of skiers were carried from Blackbushe to Salzburg and Geneva. However, during the summer of 1952 Air Transport Charter was successfully prosecuted for the operation of unlicensed flights between Blackbushe and Jersey, and all flying ceased on 31 October 1952.

## AIRWORK LTD

During the summer of 1947 Airwork Ltd operated a series of tourist flights to European destinations for the Polytechnic Touring Association, using its new fleet of Vickers Vikings. The airline went on to provide the same organisation with flights from Blackbushe to Basel under a BEA Associate Agreement and, during the winter of 1952–53, Airwork commenced a series of winter sports flights from Blackbushe for the Ski Club of Great Britain. Fourteen services were operated at weekly intervals to Stavanger in Norway, with the inclusive price of £38 covering round-trip air travel, twelve days' accommodation and meals, the hire of ski equipment and ski instruction.

## SKYWAYS LTD

In May 1946 Skyways Ltd commenced a series of 'aerial cruises' to Switzerland on behalf of the Sir Henry Lunn Travel Agency. Two services were operated each week until the end of August, using Avro York aircraft fitted with thirty red leather, non-adjustable, armchair-style seats. A two-week holiday cost £25 per person.

The programme was repeated for the summer of 1947 and in June of that year Skyways inaugurated a thrice weekly aerial cruise for Elder Dempster (Canary Islands) and Killick Martin & Co. The York aircraft departed from Northolt Airport near London and flew to Gando on Gran Canaria via Lisbon.

Then, in November 1953, the airline, now trading as Skyways of London, launched fortnightly 'Crusader' Colonial Coach low-fare services to Nicosia on Cyprus, via Malta, for £41 one way or £75 round trip. These operated from the company's new base at Stansted Airport in Essex, and once again used Avro York aircraft.

## CIRO'S AVIATION

Ciro's Aviation was founded in December 1946, and commenced operations with a working capital of £12,500 and one Dakota aircraft. The airline was run from the Ciro's Club in London's Mayfair and specialised in luxury air travel. In 1950 Pilot

Travel signed an agreement with Ciro's Aviation for the aerial transportation of its clients around Europe. Flights commenced on 1 June 1950 after two Dakotas had been hired exclusively for a twenty-week period.

Two services were operated each week to Innsbruck and then onwards to Balzano in the Italian Dolomites. The airline also carried out a sixteen-day aerial tour for Pilot Travel, which took in many cities and towns in France and Italy. Many of the passengers belonged to Catholic organisations and a tour was arranged in conjunction with them which began with a flight to Turin and a coach transfer onwards to Rome. After a week there the passengers were flown to Tarbes for a week in Lourdes before being flown home. The tour cost 67 guineas, of which £19 was for the air transportation.

Throughout 1950 Ciro's Aviation also operated inclusive tour charter flights from London to Rijeka and Salzburg, and from Birmingham to Le Touquet in France. With the approach of winter these services came to an end. With high prices being paid for good second-hand Dakotas, the company decided to sell its aircraft, and all flying had ceased by the end of January 1951.

## LANCASHIRE AIRCRAFT CORPORATION

During 1947 the Lancashire Aircraft Corporation (which was later to purchase Skyways Ltd) operated 'coach-air' holiday flights between Blackpool and the Isle of Man in conjunction with Ribble Motor Services. Coaches came from all over the north of England to connect with up to sixteen Dakota flights each day in peak season.

## BKS AEROCHARTER

On 12 October 1951 four directors of the charter airline Crewsair resigned and set up their own airline. They agreed to accept a Dakota aircraft in lieu of cash payments for their Crewsair shareholdings, and thus BKS Aerocharter was born.

The now expanded fleet of Dakotas completed five round trips to Basel through September 1952, carrying thirty-two students on each trip. At the end of that month, one Dakota was despatched to Johannesburg with twenty-nine passengers on board, operating on behalf of the South African low-fare airline, Tropic Airways.

During the winter of 1952, BKS secured contracts for eight charter flights between London and Innsbruck for the Austrian Alpine Club, and also for three 'Mediterranean Air Cruises' which lasted between eight and fifteen days and took in several Mediterranean holiday destinations. During the period February–April 1953 the airline operated five similar Mediterranean tours for US servicemen stationed in West Germany.

# 5

# The Struggle to Become Established

The decade spanning the beginning of the 1950s until the early 1960s saw many of the first holiday charter airlines expanding and flourishing (if only for a while, in some cases), and the establishment of new ones, some of whom were to become major players in the industry.

## EAST ANGLIAN FLYING SERVICES (CHANNEL AIRWAYS)

East Anglian Flying Services began life in 1946 as the brainchild of Squadron Leader R.J. 'Jack' Jones. After an initial period of scratching a living from pleasure flights the company moved into the newly opened municipal airport at Southend in January 1947 and began to build up a network of cross-Channel scheduled services.

A change of name to Channel Airways followed, and on 1 October 1956 the airline commenced services to the new airport at Rotterdam, using small de Havilland Doves. Channel Airways went on to acquire larger Bristol 170, Vickers Viking and Douglas Dakota aircraft, and during the summer of 1959 weekly inclusive tour charters were being operated from Manchester to Ostend with the Vikings.

During the 1960 summer season Vikings and Dakotas flew passengers from Southend to Basle and Ostend, where they transferred to coaches for the long onward road journeys to resorts in Switzerland, Austria and Italy. By the summer of 1962 the Vikings were also in use on tour services from Southend to Perpignan and Munich.

## TRANSAIR LTD

Transair Ltd was originally founded in February 1947 as an air taxi company based at Croydon Airport. It also built up a healthy business transporting newspapers to various points in Europe, but the airline also began carrying holidaymakers, initially for Ackroyd's Air Travel, from as early as 1948.

Dakota aircraft were introduced from February 1953, and that summer they were used to commence inclusive tour flights from Croydon to Vienna and Lourdes, and on seasonal scheduled services to the Channel Islands. The summer of 1954 saw them in use on an expanded inclusive tour network from Croydon, including flights to Alghero for Horizon Holidays.

In 1955 Transair also began flying out of Gatwick Airport to Jersey, Lourdes, Perpignan, Hamburg, Klagenfurt, Venice, Turin, Basel, Toulouse and Alghero, and from Manchester to Ostend. During the early 1950s Transair and Horizon Holidays jointly formed Pilgrim Tours to operate pilgrimage tours to the shrines at Lourdes, with an initial frequency of one Dakota flight each week. Between June and September 1955 Transair also operated nine round trips between Croydon and Basel for Methodist Guild Continental Holidays, and flights to La Baule and Biarritz for Horizon Holidays.

For the winter months of 1955–56 Transair succeeded in securing contracts for flights to the ski resorts in Austria and Switzerland, most of these arrangements being with the RAF Winter Sports Association and the Combined Services Winter Sports Association. Skiers were flown to Zurich and then transported by road to St Moritz and Zermatt. Over fifty round trips were made over a sixteen-week period.

After a busy summer 1956 programme, Transair became a wholly owned subsidiary of Airwork Ltd, but continued operations under its own name.

## AIR KRUISE LTD

In the summer of 1950 Air Kruise inaugurated its first scheduled services, from Lympne Airport in Kent to Le Touquet, Calais and Ostend. Three flights were operated each day, using De Havilland Rapide biplanes.

On 1 May 1954 Air Kruise became a part of the British Aviation Services Group, which was also operating scheduled services out of Lympne using the aircraft of another subsidiary, Silver City Airways. Two of Silver City's Dakota aircraft were transferred to Air Kruise, and two more examples were acquired in 1955. Inclusive tour flights were carried out on behalf of several tour operators, and when Lympne closed to airline services in November 1954 Air Kruise moved to Lydd Airport, also in Kent.

For the summer of 1955 holiday charters were operated from Lydd to Basel, Geneva, Turin, Venice, Salzburg, Copenhagen and Lyon, from Manchester to Geneva, and from Birmingham to Ostend and Basel, all mainly in conjunction with the tour operator, Blue Cars. Seventy-five flights were operated each week by a fleet of six Dakotas, and 40,000 passengers were carried.

In September 1955 Air Kruise announced that it had ordered 'not fewer than six' examples of the new Handley Page Herald turboprop airliner, but this order was not to be fulfilled. Instead, in 1956, three 'Wayfarer' passenger conversions of the Bristol 170 freighter were transferred from Silver City to Air Kruise, and these operated alongside Dakotas on the company's inclusive tour flight programme, which was by then the most extensive of any UK airline.

One of the largest contracts was with Blue Cars (Continental) Coach Cruises, and in January 1957 Air Kruise and Blue Cars announced a new joint venture, the Blue Arrow coach-air-rail services from London to the Côte d'Azur, the Costa Brava and the French Alps. Passengers travelled in a Blue Cars coach from London to Lydd, where they boarded an Air Kruise 'Arrow Class' flight to Lyon for onward transportation by train to their chosen resort. The services commenced in March 1957, and the through fare from London to Nice was in the region of £20, depending on the date of travel.

During 1958 the Air Kruise aircraft were gradually absorbed into the Silver City Airways fleet and the company name was dropped.

# EAGLE AVIATION LTD

On 14 April 1948 Harold Bamberg registered Eagle Aviation Ltd as an air charter company with a capital of £100. The company initially concentrated on worldwide ad hoc cargo and passenger charters out of Bovingdon (Hertfordshire) and Luton airports with a fleet of four-engined Avro Yorks, but in November 1952 it relocated again, to Blackbushe, where Viking and Dakota aircraft were now used, with the emphasis on passenger operations.

In December 1952 two tours were operated for US servicemen stationed in Europe, both of which used Dakotas. One departed from Milan for a ten-day tour around the Middle East, while another aircraft took passengers from Hamburg to Spain and the south of France. Then, on 6 June 1953, Eagle inaugurated a scheduled passenger route between Blackbushe and Belgrade after being the first British independent airline to gain approval for an international scheduled service since the Second World War.

Throughout the early 1950s the airline developed a pattern of scheduled services from Blackbushe, operating these alongside trooping contract flights. In 1953 Harold Bamberg borrowed £420,000 from a bank and purchased a fleet of fourteen Vickers Vikings from the state airline BEA, several of these being converted to a thirty-seven-seat high-density layout by an associate company, Eagle Aircraft Services Ltd. When used on civilian services these aircraft were advertised as 'Mayfair' Vikings, while the name 'Troopmaster' was adopted for aircraft operating trooping contracts.

Having acquired such a large number of aircraft, Mr Bamberg now had to find work for them all. After trying unsuccessfully to interest Thomas Cook & Son in the idea of working together on package holidays using chartered Eagle Vikings, he acquired a financial interest in the Sir Henry Lunn travel agency chain, becoming its chairman and managing director. Early in 1955 he went back to the bank and borrowed more money with which he purchased the company outright. During the summer of 1955 Eagle Aviation aircraft operated the entire Sir Henry Lunn inclusive tour programme, flying from Blackbushe to destinations such as Corsica, Klagenfurt, Minorca, Nice, Palma, Turin and Valencia with a fleet of eighteen Vikings and two Dakotas.

The summer 1956 flight programme also included services for other tour operators, such as Wenger Air Tours and the Co-operative Travel Service, and new destinations from Blackbushe including Luxembourg, Lyon, Perpignan, San Sebastian and Zagreb. That summer also saw the first Eagle inclusive tour flights from Manchester and Birmingham to Palma on behalf of Sir Henry Lunn.

It seems that 1956 was to be an eventful year for Eagle. On 18 May a Viking took off from Blackbushe for Dinard to inaugurate the first international scheduled service from a London airport to be operated by a UK independent airline in direct competition with BEA. Then, on 7 June, an Eagle Viking became the first British civil aircraft to land at Moscow since the Second World War, when it transported a party of eleven fashion models there from Blackbushe via Warsaw.

During November and December 1956 an unsuccessful uprising against the occupying Soviet regime took place in Hungary. Refugees fled across the border into Austria and Eagle joined with several other independent airlines in the operation of an airlift to carry them out of Vienna and Linz to Blackbushe. In all, 1,200 refugees were transported on thirty-six Eagle flights, more than any other British airline.

In early 1957 Eagle Airways was set up to operate the Eagle scheduled services, while Eagle Aviation continued to be responsible for inclusive tour charters, trooping flights and other general charter work.

Early in 1958 Harold Bamberg purchased Poly Travel and merged it with the Sir Henry Lunn chain to form Lunn Poly. During the summer of 1958 a fourteen-strong fleet of Vikings continued to operate inclusive tour charters from Blackbushe, Birmingham and Manchester to over twenty destinations, while flights to Dinard, Innsbruck, Basel, Jersey, La Baule, Luxembourg and Ostend were changed over to a scheduled service basis. On 8 August 1958, Eagle moved into a bigger league

↑ A Douglas DC-4 of Liverpool-based Starways departs the ramp on another inclusive tour service. (Via author)

↓ Dan-Air Ambassador G-AMAH starts up at Gatwick Airport in July 1969. (Via author)

↑ A Canadair Argonaut of Derby Airways (later to be renamed British Midland Airways) used on inclusive tour services. (Via author)

↓ Handley Page Hermes G-ALDE of Air Safaris. (Via author)

↑ Falcon Airways Hermes G-ALDC at Blackbushe Airport in the late 1950s. (Via author)

↓ Invicta Airways Douglas DC-4 G-ASPN at Liverpool Airport on a charter service in 1968. (Via author)

↑ Air Ferry Douglas DC-6A G-APNP embarks passengers for a tour service from Manchester in August 1968. (Via author)

↓ Airspeed Ambassador G-AMAE of Dan-Air Services. (Via author)

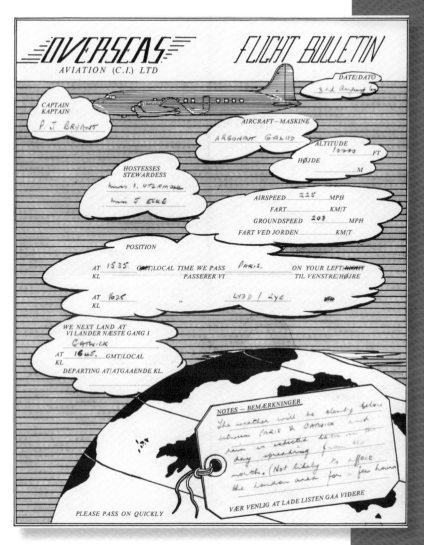

# OVERSEAS AVIATION (C.I.) LTD

## FLIGHT BULLETIN

DATE/DATO
3rd August '62

CAPTAIN
KAPTAJN
P. J. BRYANT

AIRCRAFT—MASKINE
ARGONAUT G-ALHD

ALTITUDE
HØJDE
10000 FT
_____ M

HOSTESSES
STEWARDESS
Miss I. UTERMOHL
Miss J. ESKE

AIRSPEED 225 MPH
FART _____ KM/T
GROUNDSPEED 208 MPH
FART VED JORDEN _____ KM/T

POSITION

AT 1535 GMT/LOCAL TIME WE PASS PARIS ON YOUR LEFT/RIGHT
KL PASSERER VI TIL VENSTRE/HØJRE

AT 1625 " LYDD / RYE
KL

WE NEXT LAND AT
VI LANDER NÆSTE GANG I
GATWICK
AT 1645 GMT/LOCAL
KL
DEPARTING AT/ATGAAENDE KL.
_____

NOTES — BEMÆRKNINGER
The weather will be cloudy below
between PARIS & GATWICK and
rain is expected later in the
day spreading from the
north. (Not likely to affect
the London area for a few hours

PLEASE PASS ON QUICKLY

VÆR VENLIG AT LADE LISTEN GAA VIDERE

↑ A flight bulletin issued from the flight deck of Overseas Aviation Canadair Argonaut G-ALHD for circulation among the passengers of an inclusive tour service inbound to Gatwick. (Via author)

← Channel Airways Vickers Viking G-APOP at Manchester. (Via author)

→ Handley Page Hermes G-ALDA of Air Links. (Via author)

→ One of the Euravia fleet of Lockheed Constellations at the airline's Luton base. (Via author)

→ Three of the Euravia fleet of Lockheed Constellations. (Via author)

when its first four-engined Douglas DC-6A aircraft was delivered to Blackbushe from the USA.

# DERBY AVIATION

Based initially at the grass airfield at Burnaston, near Derby, Derby Aviation was registered as an airline company on 16 February 1949. The company began airline operations with summer-only services to Jersey with De Havilland Rapide biplanes, but from April 1955 a small fleet of Dakota aircraft was also built up. For the summer of 1958 three Dakotas were in service on inclusive tour charter flights from Burnaston to Austria, Switzerland, France, Italy, Majorca and the Costa Brava on behalf of several Midlands-based tour operators.

Derby Airways was set up on 12 March 1959 to take over the airline operations and associated aircraft of Derby Aviation, and by the summer of 1959 the airline was operating holiday charters out of Birmingham, Gatwick and Manchester airports, as well as its home base at Burnaston. Winter services to Austria, Norway and Switzerland commenced later that year. Eight Dakotas were in use for the summer of 1961, and in the October Derby Airways acquired three four-engined Canadair Argonaut airliners from the liquidator of the failed Overseas Aviation. This type entered service that winter on flights from the Midlands to Tenerife.

On 7 October 1961 tragedy struck when one of the Derby Airways Dakotas crashed into Mount Canigou while carrying a party of local government officials, civil servants and their families on a charter flight from Gatwick to Perpignan on behalf of Whitehall Travel. There were no survivors.

During the 1963 summer season the Argonauts operated inclusive tour flights from Manchester to Ostend, Klagenfurt and Perpignan; from Bristol and Cardiff to Alicante, Barcelona, Palma and Tarbes; and from Birmingham to Barcelona, Cork, Ostend, Palma, Perpignan, Tarbes and Venice. The Dakotas, meanwhile, were still used for services to Ostend from Swansea, Bristol and Cardiff.

Derby Airways changed its name to British Midland Airways on 1 October 1964, and in April 1965 the airline relocated its operating base to the newly opened East Midlands Airport at Castle Donington. Sadly, on 4 June 1967, a British Midland Argonaut was on final approach to Manchester Airport with a full load of Arrowsmith Holidays passengers returning from Majorca when it crashed into a relatively empty area in the centre of Stockport, with the loss of seventy-two passengers and crew. The airline's remaining two Argonauts were withdrawn from service, but by then British Midland had introduced its first turboprop Viscount aircraft.

## STARWAYS LTD

In December 1948 an air charter company called Starways Ltd was formed by two pilots, Captain Noel Rodnight and Captain Albert Dean, with a capital of £2,000. A Percival Q6 twin-engined aircraft was acquired, and the company anticipated using this on charter flights out of Blackpool Airport, including the carriage of performers appearing at theatres in Blackpool during the summer season. However, the Q6 aircraft was destroyed in a crash in Wales in 1949 and was replaced by an Avro Anson, and that same year the company moved to Liverpool Airport.

In 1950 the first Dakota aircraft joined the fleet, and during 1951 Mr F.H. Wilson was appointed chairman. Mr Wilson was a Liverpool businessman who already owned several companies, including the Cathedral Touring Agency which was to provide Starways with all of its early inclusive tour contracts once the airline began to concentrate on this aspect of operations.

Starways was unusual among its contemporaries at this time in that it concentrated all of its activities on the north of England, Scotland and Northern Ireland, and did not seek to compete for the traffic out of the south of England.

During the summer of 1952 charter flights were operated with Dakotas from Liverpool to Jersey and Tarbes (for the shrines at Lourdes) for the Cathedral Touring Agency (CTA), while Anson aircraft were used for Saturday services to Jersey, via Gatwick. During that year three more Dakotas were introduced into service, and for the 1953 season the type also operated inclusive tour flights to Bilbao (or, occasionally, Biarritz instead).

In June 1954 Starways began flying from Glasgow to Tarbes, and from Liverpool to Nice, with the Dakotas used on this route usually having to make a refuelling stop at Bournemouth or Jersey en route.

Throughout the 1950s Starways and CTA developed an association with Catholic organisations, and worked with them on pilgrimage tours. In the summer of 1955 flights from Belfast to Tarbes were added, but the inclusive tour holiday market was not neglected either and tour flights from Liverpool to San Sebastian, via Biarritz, were inaugurated that year.

The airline began to work with other tour operators as well as CTA, and in May 1956 commenced weekly charter flights from Glasgow's Renfrew Airport to Jersey for Nugents Air Trips.

A big step up occurred at the end of 1957 when Starways took delivery of its first four-engined Douglas DC-4 aircraft. For the summer of 1958, two seventy-two-seat DC-4s were in service, being used both for inclusive tour charters and on a greatly expanded programme of pilgrimage flights to Tarbes, in the centennial year of the shrine at Lourdes. Services operated from Belfast, Liverpool and Manchester, using both DC-4s and Dakotas. Both types were also utilised on the holiday charter flights from Glasgow to Barcelona, Basel, Bergen, Bilbao, Palma, San Sebastián and Santander, and from Liverpool to Basel, Bergen, Biarritz, Bilbao, Palma and Santander. Many of the services from Glasgow also called in at Liverpool or Manchester to pick up additional passengers.

In February 1961 Starways acquired its first turboprop, a former Air France Vickers Viscount, and this joined the DC-4s and Dakotas on the summer 1961 inclusive tour flight programme which was the most extensive yet. On heavily booked flights to the Mediterranean, however, the Viscount frequently needed to make a refuelling stop at either Gatwick or Bordeaux. The summer 1962 charter programme was restricted to departures from Glasgow, Liverpool and Manchester, and was flown entirely at weekends, as by then the aircraft were also being utilised on weekday scheduled services.

On 19 November 1963, Starways signed an 'initial co-operation agreement' with British Eagle International Airlines. The services initially continued unchanged, but on 31 December 1963 British Eagle took over completely, and Starways ceased operations.

# BKS

In March 1953 the Air Transport Advisory Council granted seven-year licences to BKS Aerocharter for the operation of inclusive tour charter flights from Southend to Calvi and Palma, and from Newcastle to Basel and Paris. The flights out of Southend were operated in conjunction with Horizon Holidays and commenced in May 1953 with one round trip to each destination each week. The Dakota aircraft that were used typically cruised at around 7,500ft at 166mph, and a refuelling stop at Lyon was necessary. At that time, Horizon were offering a fourteen-day holiday in Corsica for just under £40.

At the beginning of 1954 the airline changed its name to BKS Air Transport to reflect its growing emphasis on scheduled services, but the holiday charters continued and grew, with Newcastle–Tarbes flights being added that year. For the summer of 1955, four Vickers Vikings were in service and were used on charters to Palma, Calvi and Oporto for Horizon Holidays. By the summer of 1956 BKS was operating inclusive tour flights for Roberts Tours from Newcastle, Southend and West Hartlepool airports to Milan and Nice, and from Southend to Barcelona, Basel, Cologne, Geneva, Klagenfurt, Naples, Nice, Palermo, Perpignan, Rome and San Sebastian for Sky Tourist Services.

In July 1957 BKS acquired its first Airspeed Ambassador aircraft from BEA. Two more followed, and all three aircraft were converted from their original forty-seven or forty-nine seat configuration to a new fifty-five passenger layout, using new lightweight seats supplied by Aviation Traders Engineering. For the 1958 summer season the Ambassadors participated in an extensive BKS programme of holiday charter flights from Southend to Barcelona, Basel, Calvi, Lisbon, Málaga, Naples, Nice, Palma, Perpignan and Rome.

## DAN-AIR

One of Britain's longest-lived and best-known charter airlines came into existence almost by accident in 1952 when the London shipping agency Davies & Newman became charter broker for a small airline called Meredith Air Transport. To help ease this company's financial burden, Davies & Newman agreed to take a debenture on its only aircraft, a Dakota, which set off from Southend in December 1952 with passengers bound for a fourteen-day tour of the eastern Mediterranean.

On Christmas Eve the aircraft overran the 3,900ft runway at Jerusalem and damaged its tailwheel. Meredith Air Transport was forced to charter a BKS Aerocharter Dakota to fly out a party of engineers to repair the disabled aircraft and to carry its passengers on the remainder of the tour.

The Meredith Dakota was eventually repaired and returned to service, but by May 1953 the airline was in serious financial trouble and Davies & Newman took possession of the Dakota. On 21 May 1953, they registered a new subsidiary called Dan-Air Services Ltd to operate the aircraft, using the initials of the parent company as the basis of the new airline's name.

Meredith Air Transport was contracted to manage the operations of Dan-Air for the first six months of its existence, and operations commenced in June 1953, initially using the Meredith base at Southend. The first service was a charter from Southend to Shannon, via Manchester, and for much of the summer of 1953 Dan-Air's Dakota was engaged on inclusive tour flights from Southend to Calvi, relying on ad hoc passenger and freight charter work to see it through the winter months. By the end of 1953 Dan-Air had carried 4,243 passengers.

At the beginning of 1954 Dan-Air acquired a second Dakota and transferred its main operating base to Blackbushe Airport. A subsidiary, called Dan-Air Engineering, was also set up to establish and run an engineering base at Lasham Airfield in Hampshire.

The inclusive tour flights to Calvi resumed in the summer of 1954, operating out of Blackbushe on Sundays for Fregata Travel. Charter flights for other tour operators were also operated to Biarritz, Ostend, Paris, Perpignan, Pisa and Tarbes, and by 1956 Dan-Air was flying on behalf of Arrowsmith Holidays and Mercury Travel. In June 1958 the airline inaugurated its first scheduled service route, from Blackbushe to Jersey.

Throughout its life, Dan-Air was to continue to operate a mix of scheduled service and holiday charter flights. De Havilland Heron aircraft also appeared on some inclusive tour services, and for the summer of 1959 a Bristol 170 freighter, which had been converted to a forty-four-seat 'Wayfarer' configuration, was also used for this work, including Dan-Air's first holiday charter programme out of Manchester, commencing with a service to Palma on 17 May 1959. Other destinations served from Manchester included Basel, Lyon, Ostend, Pisa and Zürich.

The Dakotas, meanwhile, were used for a small inclusive tour programme for the tour operator Motours. Each summer Saturday, the thirty-two-seater aircraft would fly a party of tourists to either Munich or Nice, returning to Gatwick that evening before repositioning empty to Blackbushe. The passengers would pick up hire cars at their arrival airport and drive at a leisurely pace to either Munich or Nice, before returning from there to Gatwick one or two weeks later.

In November 1959 Dan-Air purchased three Airspeed Ambassador aircraft, and these entered service in a forty-nine-seat layout in the summer of 1960, on holiday charters to Amsterdam, Brussels, Munich, Nice, Paris, Santander and Tours, as well as on seasonal scheduled services to Jersey and on winter sports charters to Geneva for Inghams Tours. The closure of Blackbushe Airport on 31 May 1960 resulted in the transfer of the Dan-Air operating base to Gatwick. The Dakotas were still in use, operating some tour flights from Gatwick and Manchester, as well as scheduled services within the UK, and they were also to become a familiar sight on day-trip flights to the Dutch bulb fields from many British airports.

The inclusive tour programmes were being flown almost exclusively by the Ambassadors by 1963, operating from Manchester to Basel, Ostend and Tarbes, and from Gatwick to a large number of destinations. Their excellent passenger appeal resulted in high load factors, and in addition to the normal tour flights they were also used on 'round robin' holiday tours of Greece. On these, an Ambassador would fly from Gatwick to Athens with a load of passengers. On arrival these would disembark, and the aircraft would be boarded by another party who would be flown to Rhodes for the next part of their holiday. There, another crew would take over the aircraft and fly a new group of holidaymakers to Crete, where the aircraft would pick up the passengers who had finished their tour of Greece and fly them home to Gatwick.

For the summer of 1964 an expanded flight programme out of Manchester was operated by the Ambassadors to Bordeaux, Dinard, Munich, Perpignan and Tarbes, while the Dakotas still maintained Sunday services between Manchester and Ostend.

One of the Ambassadors suffered a mishap in April 1966 while operating a Clarksons Tour flight to Beauvais. It overran the wet runway on landing and was damaged, fortunately without injury to the passengers.

# ORION AIRWAYS

Many small UK independent airlines began their existence in the late 1950s, but many of them only managed to survive for a few years. Orion Airways was founded by Captain Peter Palmer and Mrs Pamela Palmer in January 1956, Captain Palmer having previously been a director of Independent Air Travel.

For the summer of 1957 the airline increased its share capital from the initial £100 and a Vickers Viking was acquired and based at Bournemouth Airport. Operations began on 11 August 1957 with a flight from Blackbushe to Perpignan, and for the rest of the summer the aircraft was kept busy on inclusive tour charters to Barcelona, Basel, Lyon, Nice, Palma and Perpignan. By the summer of 1958 Orion employed five pilots and thirteen other staff, but the tour flight programme was still being carried out by the airline's sole aircraft.

Finally, in April 1959, a second Viking was acquired. The occasional holiday charter was operated out of Gatwick or Liverpool, but the bulk of the programme was still from Blackbushe and by the end of 1959 three Vikings were in service.

The closure of Blackbushe Airport in May 1960 led to the transfer of the Orion operating base to Gatwick Airport, and during June 1960 services were operated from there to Basel, Bordeaux, Klagenfurt, Luxembourg, Lyon, Maastricht, Perpignan, Rotterdam, Strasbourg, Tarbes and Treviso. By mid-October, however, the company's operations had been run down for the winter with the last inclusive tour flight of the year arriving at Gatwick from Palma on 30 October. Like many of its contemporaries, Orion Airways did not survive the winter, and its Vikings were eventually to pass into the hands of another charter operator, Air Safaris.

# AIR SAFARIS

The Air Safaris story really began on 29 November 1954, when Meredith Air Transport, which had remained in existence after its sole Dakota became the founder member of the Dan-Air fleet, changed its name to African Air Safaris. Earlier that year Meredith Air Transport had acquired a Vickers Viking, which had been used by the South African airline Trek Airways for low-fare flights between South Africa and Europe.

In 1958 two Trek Airways Vikings were transferred to African Air Safaris, which remained the UK sales agent for Trek. Its Vikings still flew occasional services to Johannesburg on behalf of Trek, but that year the airline began to seek out European work for the aircraft, starting with a charter flight for the Ford Motor Company, carrying twenty-six passengers from Southend to Antwerp on the evening of 30 April 1958. This trip was followed on 22 May by a charter from

← The elegant lines of a Euravia Lockheed Constellation in flight. (Via author)

← Two Eagle Aviation Vickers Vikings at Blackbushe Airport in the 1950s. (Via Peter Brown)

← Four Eagle Aviation Vikings disembarking passengers – a typical scene at Blackbushe Airport in the 1950s. (Via Peter Brown)

← Air Kruise Bristol 170 G-AIME in the maintenance area at Blackbushe Airport in the 1950s. (Via Peter Brown)

→ A late 1950s line-up of aircraft outside the terminal building at Blackbushe, with a Dan-Air Ambassador nearest the camera. (Via Peter Brown)

→ The terminal building at Blackbushe Airport, with an Independent Air Travel Viking on the tarmac. (Via Peter Brown)

→ A Blue Air Viking outside the terminal buildings at Blackbushe Airport. (Via Peter Brown)

→ A Continental Viking taxying at Blackbushe Airport. (Via Peter Brown)

← Derby Airways Dakota G-APBC at Blackbushe Airport on a tour service. (Via Peter Brown)

← An Eagle Airways Douglas DC-6A at Blackbushe Airport. (Via Peter Brown)

← Eagle Aviation Vickers Viking G-APAT at Blackbushe Airport. (Via Peter Brown)

← Eagle Aviation Vickers Viking G-AGRS at Blackbushe Airport. (Via Peter Brown)

→ Eagle Aviation Vickers Viking G-AIVC at Blackbushe. (Via Peter Brown)

→ An in-flight portrait of Eagle Airways Douglas DC-6A G-APON. (Via Peter Brown)

→ Eagle Airways Douglas DC-6A G-APON at Blackbushe Airport. (Via Peter Brown)

→ Eagle Aviation Vickers Viking G-AHPM at Blackbushe Airport. (Via Peter Brown)

Southend to Luxembourg with a group of Trek Airways passengers catching a connecting flight from there to Johannesburg.

This co-operation with Trek Airways was to continue throughout the remainder of 1958, with both African Air Safaris' Vikings operating all the way through to South Africa during the second half of the year. However, the winter of 1958–59 was a very quiet time for the airline, and the Southend Airport authorities must have had some doubts about its financial viability as they insisted on cash payment for landing fees on at least one occasion.

The spring of 1959 saw African Air Safaris operating many flights from Amsterdam to Southend with freshly cut tulips. At the beginning of June the airline transferred its main operating base to Gatwick Airport, and by the summer its two Vikings were in use on inclusive tour flights from there to Basel, Bergen, Düsseldorf, Gibraltar, Geneva, Jersey, Lyon, Munich, Nice, Palma, Perpignan, Rimini, Rotterdam, Tarbes, Toulouse and Zagreb, as well as still operating a number of services out of Southend.

One of the final services of the 1959 season involved both Vikings taking passengers from Gatwick to Palma on 4 October and bringing them home two weeks later. A change of name occurred on 26 November 1959, when Air Safaris Ltd was formed to take over the operations of African Air Safaris.

During the winter of 1959–60 Air Safaris' main source of revenue was the operation of flights to Dusseldorf and Luxembourg, carrying passengers connecting with Trek Airways services to South Africa. On one such service on 29 November 1959 a Viking was minutes into a Gatwick–Luxembourg flight when it was recalled to Gatwick to pick up a passenger who had checked in late. Within twenty minutes of landing the Viking was airborne again. Imagine that happening today!

It was around this period that Air Safaris, in conjunction with an associate company called Safari Travel, applied to the Air Transport Advisory Council for authorisation to operate a number of multi-destination tours, one of which was a four-week circular tour of Africa with an inclusive price of around £350 per head.

For the summer of 1960 the airline secured a number of lucrative inclusive tour flight contracts, and acquired a third Viking aircraft. Operations commenced with flights from Gatwick to Jersey on 20 April, to Gibraltar on 28 April, and to Zagreb on 1 May.

On 30 April 1960 Air Safaris acquired its first four-engined Handley Page Hermes airliner, and this entered service with flights from Gatwick to Milan and Rome on 6 and 7 May respectively. Shortly afterwards, however, another member of the fleet was lost when a Viking with twenty-seven passengers bound from Gatwick to Tarbes was inadvertently landed there with its main undercarriage still retracted. There were no serious injuries to passengers or crew but the aircraft was declared a write-off and a replacement had to be leased in at short notice and considerable cost.

An expanded fleet of four Vikings plus the single Hermes was in place for summer 1960, with the Hermes being mostly used on tour services out of Gatwick to Innsbruck, Munich, Naples, Nice, Perpignan, Pisa, Rimini, Rome and Treviso. A maintenance base was set up at Bournemouth Airport and inclusive tour flights were also operated out of there to Amsterdam, Jersey and Paris. On 15 August 1960 an Air Safaris aircraft operated a Bournemouth–Palma service on behalf of Falcon Airways, and the two charter airlines were subsequently to co-operate closely, often flying each other's services.

In November 1960 Air Safaris took over the air transport division of Don Everall Aviation and inherited that company's contracts for flights out of Birmingham to Basel, Malaga, Nice, Perpignan and Rimini for the Midlands-based tour operator Transglobe Ltd. Air Safaris also acquired one flyable Hermes and another for spares from Falcon Airways, and purchased further Vikings during the winter of 1960–61.

For the summer of 1961 Air Safaris operated inclusive tour flights out of Birmingham, Bournemouth, Gatwick, Glasgow, Manchester and Newcastle to numerous Mediterranean resorts. The flights from Newcastle went to Barcelona, Palma, Perpignan, Rimini, Tarbes and Valencia for Horizon Travel and Airway Holidays, but the airline's biggest contracts for 1961 were for services out of Gatwick for Horizon Travel and Universal Sky Tours.

With an eye to future expansion, Air Safaris received demonstrations of both the Handley Page Herald and Avro 748 turboprop aircraft during 1961, and from July–September 1961 the company applied for 120 B Licences for tour flight services during the coming winter. However, before it would consider granting the licences the ATLB required that the airline's finances be strengthened, and Air Safaris was unable to secure the necessary credit.

During August and September 1961 Air Safaris had obtained extra revenue from the operation of flights on behalf of the large charter airline, Overseas Aviation, but that company then ran into financial problems and this line of work dried up. Air Safaris' operations were cut back and on 31 October 1961 a Hermes landed at Gatwick from Lisbon on the final service of the 1961 season.

Efforts were made to find the money to keep the airline going, but these were unsuccessful and Air Safaris officially ceased operating on 2 November 1961. At that time the airline had debts totalling £521,073, of which over £100,000 was owed to Esso for fuel. Most of the aircraft were eventually ferried back to Bournemouth for sale or scrapping, and on 11 January 1962 all of the airline's licences were revoked.

## INDEPENDENT AIR TRAVEL

Independent Air Travel began life not as an airline but as a travel agency, being registered as such on 1 January 1953. In August 1953 the company made a brief foray into air transport operations when it purchased an Avro Anson aircraft and based it at Southend Airport. However, this machine appears to have only operated one revenue service, from Blackbushe to Amsterdam in October 1953, before it was disposed of in February 1954. Independent Air Travel then reverted to travel agency operations until February 1955, when it was purchased by Captain Marian Kozubski and a group of fellow airline pilots.

Captain Kozubski had previously been chief pilot with the William Dempster charter airline and had spent much of 1954 flying Dakotas for Dan-Air Services, before joining Trek Airways and piloting Vikings on low-fare services between South Africa and Europe. The new Independent Air Travel management had secured financial backing from Captain 'Ted' Langton, who had set up his own holiday company called Universal Sky Tours, and the intention was for Independent Air Travel to carry all of his tour passengers.

Independent's operations began in a modest fashion, using small De Havilland Dove aircraft on general freight and passenger charters, which included a contract to fly passengers to Paris on behalf of the Welsh airline, Cambrian Air Services. By January 1956, however, the Doves had been disposed of and Independent had purchased its first Vickers Viking. By early May of that year three Vikings were in service. One was operated from Stockholm and Malmo on behalf of a Swedish charter airline and the other two were used on holiday charters from Blackbushe to destinations such as Barcelona, Basel, Madrid, Palma and Valencia for Universal Sky Tours, and also on inclusive tour flights out of Dusseldorf for various West German tour operators.

The Independent base at Blackbushe at this time consisted of three caravans, two prefabricated huts and a check-in desk situated in the terminal building. A maintenance base was also established at Bournemouth Airport. During the winter of 1956–57 a further five Vikings were acquired, with one being allocated to a regular series of tourist and student charters between Blackbushe and Basle on behalf of Swiss Universal Air Charter.

For the summer of 1957 a fleet of six Vikings was in service on an extensive tour flight programme out of Blackbushe, holiday charters from Southend to Barcelona, Basel and Palma, pilgrimage flights to Tarbes, and charters from Manchester to Barcelona, Palma and Valencia for Universal Sky Tours.

During 1957, Independent purchased two four-engined Douglas DC-4s, and these larger aircraft gave the airline the ability to operate charter flights to the Far East, Africa and North America, as well as to the Mediterranean area. On 31 December 1957 one of the DC-4s, under the command of Captain Marian

Kozubski, was en route from Dusseldorf to Singapore on a Ministry of Defence cargo charter flight. The next planned stop was at Damascus, but the aircraft was intercepted by Albanian jet fighters and forced to land at Valonia in Albania. The crew were alleged to have violated Albanian airspace, but were well treated and after a few days they were allowed to fly the aircraft back to Bournemouth.

In preparation for the summer 1958 season a large number of inclusive tour contracts were negotiated, the workforce was expanded to 400 people and a fleet of three DC-4s and six Vikings was built up. However, problems were on the horizon, and in April Independent Air Travel and seven of its captains were fined £450 at Bournemouth Crown Court for infringements of the regulations governing crew rest hours and duty periods.

Then, on 2 September 1958, one of the airline's Vikings suffered engine trouble fifteen minutes after taking off from Heathrow on the first leg of a cargo charter flight to Tel Aviv for the Israeli airline, El Al. One of the Viking's engines was shut down and its propeller 'feathered' to reduce drag, but the crew could not then maintain altitude. They tried to head for Blackbushe but lost track of their position. The aircraft crashed into a house in Kelvin Gardens, Southall, and all three crew members and four people on the ground were killed.

An enquiry into the crash was held in March 1959. Captain Kozubski resigned on the first day of the inquiry, which severely criticised Independent's maintenance procedures and its systems for checking crew competence. As a result of the negative publicity arising from the enquiry's findings Universal Sky Tours transferred some of its summer 1959 flight programme to other charter airlines, and Independent began to trade under the alternative name of Blue Air. Its aircraft were either repainted with Blue Air titles or carried no airline name at all.

Despite its problems the airline still carried out a busy summer programme of inclusive tour charters from Blackbushe and other airports around the UK, but as autumn approached its operations were run down. The last two Vikings in service were ferried to the Bournemouth maintenance base on 16 October 1959, and the company then ceased trading. It had run up large debts, and its financial problems had been added to by the refusal of its insurers to honour a claim for £26,000 for the loss of the Viking that had crashed at Southall.

## FALCON AIRWAYS

When Captain Marian Kozubski resigned from Independent Air Travel in March 1959 he took a number of the airline's employees with him, and during that same month he set up Falcon Airways, with a share capital of £10,000 and an initial fleet of one Beech 18 aircraft and one Vickers Viking. Inclusive tour charter operations began on 27 March 1959 using the Viking, and during the summer this aircraft was joined by a Hermes aircraft on services which included flights for Sky Tours (previously known as Universal Sky Tours) which had originally been contracted to Independent Air Travel.

When Blackbushe Airport closed on 31 May 1960 Falcon Airways transferred its operating base to Gatwick. From there, inclusive tour flights were operated to Barcelona, Basel, Bordeaux, Copenhagen, Dusseldorf, Lyon, Maastricht, Malaga, Milan, Munich, Nice, Perpignan, Rome, Tangier, Treviso and Valencia, and charters were also flown out of Southend and Manchester.

In addition to flights for Sky Tours, the Falcon Airways Hermes also carried passengers for Trans-Alp, and for Flightways, who used the aircraft for tours to Italy, Spain, Morocco and Corsica. However, the aircraft's service ended abruptly on 9 October 1960 when it was landing at Southend from Barcelona and overran the runway due to aquaplaning. The aircraft struck an earth bank and came to rest with its tail in the air and its nose lying across the railway line that ran past the airport boundary. None of the seventy-one Sky Tours passengers and five crew were seriously injured, but the aircraft was written off and a DC-4 had to be leased in to complete the Sky Tours contract.

At the end of the 1960 season Falcon Airways disposed of its remaining aircraft and handed back its Air Operator's Certificate to the Ministry of Aviation for the winter months. During the winter the airline lay dormant, but in early 1961 Captain Kozubski went to the USA and purchased four Lockheed Constellation airliners. Three arrived in the UK and stayed there, but the fourth went on to Vienna where it was registered to an Austrian subsidiary of the airline.

Major contracts were negotiated with Sky Tours for the summer 1961 season, but because of objections from the authorities over the operation of the Austrian-registered Constellation from the UK only one Falcon Airways aircraft was available for the summer flights. Many of the Sky Tours services had to be transferred to other airlines, and a Constellation had to be hired from Trans European Airways to make up the capacity shortfall.

In July 1961 Falcon Airways received adverse press coverage when eighty-two Sky Tours passengers on a holiday to Majorca from Gatwick had their departure delayed for over twenty-four hours. The Falcon Airways aircraft had become unserviceable and the passengers were eventually taken into London to spend the night in a West End hotel. When they arrived back at Gatwick the next morning they were informed that the flight was still delayed and that it was hoped to get them away by 10 p.m. that night. Because of the problems with their own aircraft, Falcon Airways had chartered an aircraft from the French airline UAT, but had neglected to obtain a new diplomatic clearance for this aircraft and the Spanish authorities refused permission for the UAT aircraft to be used under the original clearance. The passengers eventually arrived in Palma on the original Falcon aircraft, after its technical problems had been rectified.

Falcon Airways' Constellation operations were not confined to Europe. On 28 March 1961 it took off from Georgetown in British Guiana on a charter to Gatwick with sixty-eight West Indian immigrants. Bad weather forced a landing at Stephenville, Newfoundland, and after setting off again the following day the aircraft was obliged to make another weather diversion to Gander.

By then, one of the babies among the passengers was sick and the aircraft's captain decided to fly direct from Gander to London, in contravention of the flight plan filed, in order to shorten the journey. However, the aircraft did not have sufficient dinghies on board for such a long sea crossing, and its LORAN long-range navigation system was unserviceable.

The flight arrived safely, but on 6 September 1961 Captain Kozubski appeared in court to face seven charges levelled against the airline. The aircraft captain was fined £175, Falcon Airways was fined £125 and they were each ordered to pay 50 guineas in costs.

On 19 September 1961 Falcon Airways operated its last commercial service, from Palma to Gatwick. Two days later the company's Air Operator's Certificate was withdrawn, and the airline was placed into liquidation on 2 January 1962.

## OVERSEAS AVIATION

Overseas Aviation (Channel Islands) Ltd was registered in Jersey in February 1958 to operate passenger and freight charters out of a base at Southend Airport. The airline (usually referred to as Overseas Aviation) was one of thirty-eight companies in the Overseas Group, which had grown out of a small car distribution and finance agency set up in Germany in 1949 by Ronald Myhill, a former RAF pilot. Mr Myhill had also co-founded Autair Ltd, Britain's first independent commercial helicopter operator, in 1954.

At around the same time as he established Overseas Aviation he also became chairman of Continental Air Services, although the two airlines were operated independently, and he also became involved in the formation of the Danish airline Flying Enterprise, the Dutch airline Martins Air Charter, and the Belgian airline Aviameer. The aircraft of these companies were often to be interchanged with those of Overseas Aviation. Among the first directors of Overseas were two Southend-based BKS Aerocharter pilots, and the airline's fleet maintenance was initially contracted out to BKS Engineering at Southend.

Full charter operations were launched on 1 March 1958, using a fleet of three Vikings supplemented occasionally by one owned by Swiss Universal Air Charter. A sales office was set up in Frankfurt to tap into the lucrative West German holiday charter market and Overseas was soon awarded contracts by a number of major German tour operators. Two Vikings were ferried out to Germany in March and

← Vickers Viking G-AIJE of Independent Air Travel at Blackbushe Airport. (Via Peter Brown)

← Orion Airways Vickers Viking G-AGRS is towed across the Blackbushe Airport tarmac. (Via Peter Brown)

← Vickers Viking G-AHOS of Orion Airways at Blackbushe Airport. (Via Peter Brown)

← Orion Airways Vickers Viking G-AHOS in the snow at Blackbushe Airport. (Via Peter Brown)

→ Falcon Airways Handley Page Hermes G-ALDC at Blackbushe. (Via Peter Brown)

→ Falcon Airways Vickers Viking G-AHPG taxying at Blackbushe Airport. (Via Peter Brown)

→ An Independent Air Travel Douglas DC-4 being serviced at Blackbushe Airport. (Via Peter Brown)

→ Independent Air Travel Vickers Viking G-AHPR at Blackbushe Airport. (Via Peter Brown)

← Pegasus Airlines Vickers Viking G-AHPL running up its engines at Blackbushe Airport. (Via Peter Brown)

← Pegasus Airlines Vickers Viking G-AHPL at Blackbushe Airport. (Via Peter Brown)

← Tradair Vickers Viking G-AIXR at Blackbushe Airport. (Via Peter Brown)

← Silver City Airways Bristol 170 G-AIFV in the maintenance area at Blackbushe Airport. (Via Peter Brown)

↑ Autair Vickers Viking G-AHPB taxying at Berlin (Templehof) Airport. (Ralf Mantufel)

↓ Autair Ambassador G-ALZS on final approach to Berlin (Templehof) Airport. (Ralf Mantufel)

↑ Autair Ambassador G-ALZS taxying at Berlin (Templehof) Airport. (Ralf Mantufel)

↓ Air Links Canadair Argonaut G-ALHI taxying at Berlin (Templehof) Airport. (Ralf Mantufel)

→ Autair Ambassador G-ALZS taxying at Berlin (Templehof) Airport. (Ralf Mantufel)

→ Dan-Air Dakota G-AMSS at Gatwick, after the airline had transferred operations there on the closure of Blackbushe. (Via author)

→ A Skyways of London Lockheed Constellation runs up its engines in front of the primitive early passenger facilities at Luton Airport. (Andrew Read)

→ A Euravia Lockheed Constellation aircraft. (Via author)

April, and the first charters out of Frankfurt were operated over the weekend of 12–13 April 1958.

Early services out of Hamburg took holidaymakers to Barcelona and Palma, and other flights were operated from West Berlin and Munich to destinations such as Lyon and Perpignan. Meanwhile, two Vikings remained stationed at Southend and were used on regular services to Basel for Swiss Universal Air Charter.

On 1 November 1958 Overseas Aviation took delivery of the first of a fleet of former BOAC Canadair Argonaut four-engine airliners. These had been acquired not only to offer more capacity on the inclusive tour services but also to hopefully allow expansion into the long-haul charter market. The first commercial service by the Argonauts was operated from Southend to Lisbon on 5 November 1958, and on 2 December a company called Trans Africa Air Coach was set up to operate low-fare flights to Africa.

In January 1959 an Argonaut was ferried to Copenhagen to operate a charter to the Far East for a Danish travel agency, eventually arriving back at Southend on 6 February. A week later, an Argonaut departed Southend with thirty-two passengers on a Trans Africa Air Coach service to Lourenço Marques, via Lisbon, and at the beginning of March an Argonaut carried passengers to Rio de Janeiro.

On 16 March 1959 Overseas launched a regular series of charters between Copenhagen and Palma, One week later, Viking aircraft were used to open a new season of holiday flights out of West Germany, but by May these aircraft had mostly been superseded by the larger Argonauts. For the summer of 1959, Overseas had five Argonauts and three Vikings in service, and on 29 May a new contract with Sky Tours began with a Viking tour flight from Manchester to Palma, via Toulouse. During the summer, regular weekend services were operated from Manchester to Barcelona, Palma and Treviso.

When the passenger loads were heavy or the winds were unfavourable the Vikings usually had to make a refuelling stop at Munich en route to Treviso, and the Barcelona and Palma services usually refuelled at Lyon. On the return legs it was sometimes possible to make the trip non-stop, but the Treviso–Manchester flights took around six and a half hours, while those from Barcelona took about an hour less.

Long-distance charter flights by the Argonauts continued, and in September 1959 one of these aircraft transported most of the Czechoslovakian Philharmonic Orchestra from Prague to Australasia for concerts in Auckland, Christchurch, Melbourne, Sydney and Brisbane. The Argonauts were also much in evidence on holiday flights from the UK to North Africa, Italy and Yugoslavia, and were also used along with Vikings on summer flights from West Germany to the Mediterranean.

For the summer of 1960 Overseas had a fleet of six sixty-five-seat Argonauts and six Vikings, and could also call upon the services of three Flying Enterprise

Argonauts at peak periods. There were 187 personnel on the payroll. On 12 June 1960 a scheduled passenger service between Southend and Ostend was inaugurated, with three Viking round trips being rostered for each Sunday until September. Eight days later the airline began a series of charter flights carrying students from Gothenburg to Southend. This programme continued until the end of August 1960, and on some days as many as four Argonauts were in use.

By now Overseas had outgrown its maintenance facilities at Southend and transferred its main base to Gatwick Airport where, on 14 June 1960, Geoffrey Ripon MP, the Parliamentary Secretary to the Minister of Aviation, opened the airline's new £300,000 hangar. This was of Scandinavian design and wooden construction, and at that time was the largest (at 150ft) clear-span timber building in the UK.

It was during the summer of 1960 that Overseas Aviation operated inclusive tour services from Belfast and Glasgow for the first time, but in order to fill the Argonaut aircraft it was often necessary to combine departure points. Flights from Belfast often routed via Manchester, Birmingham or Gatwick, and during July 1960 Belfast–Rimini services stopped to pick up additional passengers at both Glasgow and Gatwick.

The smaller Vikings flew twice weekly from Manchester to Ostend, and services from the airline's new base at Gatwick commenced on 25 May with a Viking charter to Luxembourg and two Argonaut flights to Vienna. For the summer 1961 season Overseas operated services from Gatwick to Basel, Copenhagen, Luxembourg, Nice, Ostend, Palma, Perpignan, Rimini, Rome, Tangier, Tunis, Vienna and Zagreb. The Argonauts were once again active on long-haul charter flights, operating during the year from Southend to Lourenço Marques for the Overseas Visitors Club, and from Gatwick on Trans Africa Air Coach services. They were even utilised on ad hoc transatlantic charter flights, and on the night of 2–3 November 1960 no less than three Argonauts were airborne over the Atlantic on eastbound return legs.

By the summer of 1961 the inclusive tour programme had become so intensive that at Manchester Airport alone four Argonauts were committed to this work at peak season weekends. In order to expand its fleet quickly and at minimum cost, on 1 June 1961 Overseas Aviation purchased fifteen Canadair North Star airliners from Trans Canada Airlines at a total cost of under £300,000, including spares. These aircraft were basically similar to the airline's former BOAC Argonauts but were furnished with only sixty seats. An initial batch of eight was delivered to Gatwick, and the first ones were pressed into service immediately as they were, but some later arrivals were soon converted to a seventy-seat layout.

On 31 July 1961 Overseas Aviation diversified into UK domestic scheduled service operations when it inaugurated a no-reservations, walk-on service between Prestwick and Gatwick via Manchester on three days each week. Passenger loads were poor, however, and the service was suspended after only eleven flights had been made and just over 100 passengers carried.

At an Air Transport Licensing Board hearing for a scheduled service between Gatwick and Porto Santo, near Madeira, the critical financial situation of Overseas Aviation was revealed for the first time. Within two weeks BP had cut off further supplies of fuel because of the non-payment of outstanding bills. On the following day a further setback occurred when a Viking departing Lyon after an intermediate stop on a Palma–Gatwick service experienced a loss of power in both engines shortly after take-off and was force-landed near Lyon Airport, fortunately without casualties.

The Overseas fleet could only keep operating for as long as its stockpiled fuel lasted. The final day of UK-based operations was 15 August 1961, when a North Star flew from Gatwick to Lyon to pick up the stranded passengers from the crashed Viking. On 22 August the 200 engineers employed by the airline's subsidiary, Overseas Aviation Engineering (GB), stopped work, and three days later they occupied the hangar at Gatwick. Services out of West Germany were able to continue for a short while longer using one Argonaut and one Viking, but these ceased when the last operational Viking returned to Southend from Hamburg on 7 October 1961.

At the time of the airline's collapse, tour operators such as Arrowsmith Holidays, Swiss Travel Service, Poly Travel and Panorama Holidays had over 5,000 clients booked to fly home from holiday on Overseas Aviation. They were obliged to charter aircraft from other airlines at premium prices to bring their clients home. In all, over £500,000 was owed to the airline's creditors, which included Rolls-Royce (for the overhaul of Merlin engines), BOAC (outstanding payment instalments on the Argonaut fleet), BP and the Inland Revenue. At the height of the 1961 summer season Overseas Aviation had been operating the second-largest fleet of any UK independent airline.

# PEGASUS AIRLINES

Not all of the holiday charter airlines of the 1950s and 1960s grew to be the size of Overseas Aviation. Typical of the smaller companies was Pegasus Airlines, which was founded in early 1958 by Mr Cyril G. Claydon, a Luton builder. On 29 May 1958 the airline's first aircraft, a Vickers Viking, arrived at its Luton Airport base, and was used that summer on inclusive tour flights from Luton and Blackbushe airports.

By the summer of 1959 three Vikings were in service on tour flights from Blackbushe to Basel, Lyon, Nice, Ostend, Palma, Perpignan and Tarbes. The Vikings also operated weekend charter flights from Luton to Jersey, and inclusive tour services from Glasgow's Renfrew Airport to destinations such as Bergen, Jersey and Ostend. When the booked loads out of Glasgow were light, departure points were often combined and a stop made at Blackbushe to pick up more passengers.

When Blackbushe closed at the end of May 1960 Pegasus transferred its main base to Gatwick, but in August of that year its operating base was relocated once again, this time to Blackpool Airport. To provide a source of revenue during the winter months a scheduled passenger service between Blackpool and Gatwick was inaugurated on 7 October 1960, and for the summer of 1961 inclusive tour flights were operated out of Gatwick. However, during the last week of October 1961 the airline's owner, Mr Claydon, announced that Pegasus Airlines was to cease operations, stating that although the company had not been losing money it had not been making any either.

Inclusive tour services ended on 23 October 1961 when two Vikings operated from Gatwick to Palma and back, and two days later the Blackpool–Gatwick scheduled service also came to an end. Between fifty and sixty aircrew and ground staff at Blackpool and Gatwick were given one week's notice. Mr Claydon was quoted as saying, 'We don't have any business between now and Easter and we cannot afford to keep the dismissed staff on. After all, we are in business – not a charity organisation.'

## CONTINENTAL AIR SERVICES

Another small charter operator of the period was Continental Air Services, which also traded as Continental Air Transport and was registered on 2 November 1957. This airline chose the Vickers Viking as its initial aircraft, commencing operations with a single aircraft on inclusive tour charters from Rotterdam to Mediterranean resorts in the summer of 1958. Two more Vikings were added that year, and services were operated out of Blackbushe to destinations which included Basel, Palma, Paris, Perpignan and Tarbes. By the summer of 1959 two more Vikings had joined the fleet.

An office was opened in London, and charters were flown out of Blackbushe, Rotterdam and Southend. Two examples of the four-engined Douglas DC-4 airliner were acquired in November 1959 and May 1960, and these were used during the summer of 1960 on inclusive tour charters out of Southend and on regular flights from Manchester to Barcelona and Palma. The Vikings were also kept busy on holiday flights out of Southend to Barcelona, Basel, Brussels, Ostend, Palma, Paris, Perpignan, Rimini, Rotterdam and Tarbes, as well as charters from Manchester and services from Glasgow to Jersey and Ostend.

However, all was not well with the company's finances and at the beginning of October 1960 one of the Vikings was impounded at Southend for non-payment of bills. The airline's final inclusive tour service was operated from Malta to Birmingham by a Viking on 2 October 1960, and on the following day the company went into voluntary liquidation with reported debts totalling over £200,000.

The airline's directors blamed the collapse on problems with aircraft serviceability. Around 40,000 passengers had been carried during the 1960 summer season but because of technical problems Continental had been forced to subcharter flights out to other airlines and had lost a considerable amount of money in the process.

## TRANS EUROPEAN AIRWAYS

Trans European Airways was founded in early 1959 as a charter operator with various small aircraft based at Fairwood Common Aerodrome near Swansea. During 1960 the company transferred its base to Coventry Airport, and at the end of that year a Bristol 170 aircraft was acquired. This type was usually employed as a freighter, but this particular example did not have the nose-loading doors fitted to most of those built and was operated as a passenger aircraft by Trans European.

The decision was taken to move up to longer-range aircraft and to enter the inclusive tour market, and in July 1961 a former Falcon Airways Lockheed Constellation entered service, flying holiday charters to Malaga, Nice and Perpignan. Inclusive tour operations continued throughout the summer and, during the winter that followed, the airline applied for licences to operate inclusive tour charters to Barcelona, Palma, Pisa and Rimini in 1962.

These applications were initially rejected by the Air Transport Licensing Board, but early in 1962 a large City group purchased a financial interest in Trans European, boosting its share capital to £75,000. By the summer of 1962 contracts had been awarded for the operation of charter flights out of West Berlin on behalf of several German travel agencies and student organisations, and for holiday flights out of Gatwick.

The 1962 season started as planned, but in late July Trans European was forced to appoint a receiver. All operations ceased in August 1962 after one of the airline's Constellations was impounded in Israel and the other fleet members suffered a similar fate at Gatwick. The company was placed into liquidation with debts totalling £125,000.

## BRITISH WESTPOINT AIRLINES

British Westpoint Airlines began life in 1961 as Westpoint Aviation, and during that summer inclusive tour charters were operated from Gatwick to Dieppe, Innsbruck and Nice with Dakota aircraft. During September and October 1961 charter flights from Gatwick to Jersey, Lyon, Maastricht, Munich, Perpignan and Tarbes were operated, along with services from Gatwick to Paris (Le Bourget) Airport, which received two round trips daily at peak periods.

From 1963 the inclusive tour work began to be phased out as the airline concentrated more on domestic scheduled services and subcontract work for other carriers including Air France. By the end of 1964 the inclusive tour flights out of Gatwick had ended, and British Westpoint ceased operations in May 1966.

## EROS AIRLINES

On 2 March 1962 Mr A. Homotas, the owner and managing director of Cyprus Travel Ltd, launched Eros Airlines (UK). The new airline started life with a capital of £20,000 and a base at Gatwick Airport, with one office in the main terminal building and another in the southern 'finger' of the terminal, this latter office having been formerly occupied by the defunct Falcon Airways. A fleet of three Vickers Vikings was acquired from the receiver of another failed airline, Air Safaris.

Eros was to be the last Gatwick-based operator of Viking aircraft, and was, in fact, the thirteenth owner of one of the examples in its fleet. During March 1962 ten pilots and six flight attendants were recruited. Among the pilots were five captains with a total of 70,000 flying hours and 120 years of flying experience between them. Operations commenced on 31 March 1962, and destinations served that summer included Barcelona, Basel, Lyon, Perpignan and Tarbes.

As autumn approached the company announced plans to introduce four-engined Douglas DC-6B airliners from October 1962 and placed a provisional order for a new Avro 748 turboprop aircraft, but neither of these hopes came to fruition. In November 1962 Mr Homotas publicly expressed his frustration with the lack of co-operation his airline was receiving from the authorities at Gatwick. Eros was not permitted to do its own ground handling at the airport as this activity was reserved for the already established airlines there, so he had to contract it out to Dan-Air Services.

The company was barred from operating one-off charter flights between the hours of 9 a.m. and 11 a.m. at weekends, and Mr Homotas was also upset by what he saw as the preferential treatment given to foreign airlines during peak periods at Gatwick, even though they did not use the airport during the unprofitable winter months.

When he applied to the Air Transport Licensing Board for route licences for the 1963 summer season he ran into more difficulties. The board was prepared to grant nine licences, but only if he increased the airline's share capital by £15,000 plus the value of the three Vikings by 14 November 1962. He was unable to comply fully, as it transpired that the Vikings were only leased, but nevertheless Eros was granted licences for holiday charter flights from Gatwick to Basel/Zurich, Munich, Perpignan and Rotterdam and also from Manchester to Basel and Ostend. This programme of flights was carried out by a reduced complement of two Vikings.

The winter of 1963–64 was a very quiet time for the airline, with its aircraft sometimes sitting idle at Gatwick for weeks at a time. Eros recommenced inclusive tour services on 13 March 1964 but these were only short-lived as the company ceased operations on 4 April that year.

## AIR LINKS

One small airline that was destined to go on to bigger things before its eventual collapse was Air Links, which was established on 21 August 1958. In May 1959 the company acquired a former Aer Lingus Dakota aircraft which was used on ad hoc charters from the airline's Gatwick base and was also leased out to other operators. A second Dakota joined Air Links in July 1961 and inclusive tour flights commenced that summer, with services being operated from Gatwick to Amsterdam, Basel, West Berlin, Dinard, Dublin, Le Havre, Le Touquet, Nice, Paris (Le Bourget) and Vichy.

In 1962 a four-engined Handley Page Hermes which had previously served with Air Safaris was acquired, and during the summer of 1963 this aircraft was operated in an eighty-two-seat layout on holiday charters to Basel, Lyon, Nice, Perpignan, Rimini and Rome. By then both Dakotas had been retired and Air Links needed more passenger capacity. Although the Hermes carried 10,329 inclusive tour passengers during the summer of 1963 it was the last flyable example in the world and so the airline had to find another similar-sized aircraft.

In March 1964 the company's first ex-BOAC Canadair Argonaut entered service, and by the summer two of these four-engined airliners were operating alongside the solitary Hermes. Air Links was eventually to operate four Argonauts, converted to a seventy-eight-seat configuration.

As well as operating out of Gatwick, Air Links also flew a small number of services from Glasgow to Palma and Perpignan, and the Hermes was still to be seen on fortnightly flights from Manchester to these same destinations. It also appeared at the 1964 Biggin Hill Air Fair, operating pleasure flights for planeloads of appreciative passengers (including the author). Its days were numbered, however, and on 13 October 1964 it landed back at Gatwick from Pakistan, via Brindisi, after completing the last commercial Hermes service. It was later ferried to Southend and scrapped, but Air Links itself was to undergo major expansion in the next few years.

## TRADAIR

In November 1957 Tradair was registered and a base was set up at Southend Airport. In February 1958 two Vickers Vikings were acquired. These were converted to a high-density thirty-six-seat layout and freight doors were also installed to ensure maximum flexibility of use. Commercial services began with a variety of ad hoc charters to destinations such as Antwerp and Rotterdam, and the airline commenced inclusive tour operations on 23 May 1958 with a flight to Basel.

Night flights from Southend to Palma, via a refuelling stop at Lyon, began on 30–31 May, and during the following month services to Perpignan and Pisa were added. Fortnightly charter flights from Southend to Malta, via Nice, commenced later that summer. In August 1958 three Vikings which had previously served with the Queen's Flight joined the fleet, and the summer season wound up with a flight back to Southend from Perpignan on 24 October.

During the winter of 1958–59 the Vikings were utilised on leisurely 'aerial cruises' such as the one which carried twenty passengers around North Africa, Spain and the Canary Islands for three weeks in November 1958. Freight charters were also carried out, and in May 1959 two more Vikings were acquired, bringing the fleet total to seven. During the spring of 1959 charter flights from Bournemouth, Southend and Stansted airports carried passengers to the Dutch bulb fields. Pilgrimage flights to Tarbes were operated during the year, and the summer inclusive tour programme included Basel, Ostend and the usual Mediterranean resorts, as well as destinations further afield such as Tenerife, Gibraltar and Casablanca. Tradair would soon need to look for larger and more modern aircraft to serve its future requirements.

## AIR FERRY

During May and June 1961 Wing Commander Hugh Kennard and his wife, Audrey, who had together founded Air Kruise in the immediate post-war years, and Lewis Leroy of the long-established coach tour operator, Leroy Tours, set up a new airline called Air Ferry. The airline was to be a subsidiary of Leroy Tours and during 1962 the two organisations applied together for a number of B Licences for inclusive tours to be based around Air Ferry flights from Manston Airport in Kent.

Two Vickers Vikings and a Douglas DC-4 were purchased for this purpose and the new airline's inaugural service took place on 30 March 1963, when forty-eight Leroy Tours clients departed Manston for Perpignan. Twenty-one passengers disembarked there and the remainder were then carried onward to Ibiza via a stop at Palma to clear Spanish customs.

In its first seven months of operations Air Ferry carried some 120,000 passengers on behalf of tour operators such as Blue Cars, Page & Moy, Clarksons and Hards Travel, as well as Leroy Tours. During the summer of 1963 DC-4 aircraft in an eighty-four-seat configuration transported holidaymakers to Basel, Dijon, Naples, Palma, Perpignan, Pisa and Verona at weekends, while the forty-two-seat Vikings flew to Basel, Dusseldorf, Le Touquet and Ostend.

By 1964 Air Ferry had five Vikings and three DC-4s in service. Ostend was one of the most popular destinations. During the course of the year 1,326 visits were made by the Air Ferry fleet, and on one particular date twenty-one round trips to Ostend were completed in a single day. Along with many other travel companies, Leroy Tours were also offering day trips to the Dutch bulb fields, flying with Air Ferry from Manston to Rotterdam at an inclusive cost of 8 guineas. The company also offered a fifteen-day 'Highlights of Yugoslavia' tour for 47 guineas, using Air Ferry aircraft for travel to Luxembourg, where onward coach transportation awaited.

In October 1964 Air Ferry was purchased by the Air Holdings Group, the parent company of British United Airways. Hugh Kennard and his wife resigned and immediately began making plans to start up a rival airline at Manston. Air Ferry continued to trade under its own name for several years, but was to lose a number of inclusive tour contracts to Hugh Kennard's new airline in 1965.

Worse was to come. A DC-4 was lost while operating a freight flight in January 1967, and in June of that year another example crashed in the Pyrenees while approaching Perpignan on an inclusive tour service from Manston. Air Ferry went on to operate more modern Douglas DC-6A and Viscount aircraft, but its fleet and identity was absorbed into British United Airways at the end of 1968.

## INVICTA AIRWAYS

Following his departure from Air Ferry in October 1964, Hugh Kennard set up a new airline called Invicta Airways. During the winter of 1964–65 a number of inclusive tour contracts were signed with companies which included Blue Cars, Page & Moy and Lumb's Tours.

Like Air Ferry, Invicta Airways elected to commence operations with Viking and DC-4 aircraft, and to base them at Manston, but securing accommodation there proved difficult as the existing passenger terminal and hangar were not available to them. Suitable sites for a new terminal and hangar were found on the east side of the airfield and the Ministry of Defence (which owned Manston as it was still an RAF base) was successfully approached for permission to erect the buildings there.

Contracts for the construction of them using preformed concrete were issued after a tendering process, and the terminal building was completed in the short time of around six weeks, being opened in time for Easter 1965. The construction of the hangar, however, was to take considerably longer, and in the meantime Invicta's engineers had to utilise an old wartime Loom hangar on the extreme western perimeter of the airfield. Another wartime RAF structure, the Parachute Building, served as the chief engineer's office, and also housed technical records, a crew room, an operations section and some toilets.

In February 1965 Invicta's first aircraft, two Vikings and two Douglas DC-4s, were acquired and the airline's first revenue service, an inclusive tour flight from Manston to Basel, took place. During that summer 120,143 passengers were conveyed from Manston to destinations that included Basel, Dusseldorf, Luxembourg, Malaga, Ostend, Palma, Perpignan, Rotterdam and Seville. Three more DC-4s and two more Vikings were purchased in time for the 1966 season, which opened with springtime flights from Manston and Glasgow to Rotterdam for the Dutch bulb fields.

These popular charter flights were repeated in 1967, and in that year Invicta inaugurated a daily scheduled passenger service between Manston and Ostend. During the summer of 1967 the airline began operating inclusive tour flights from several UK regional airports in addition to Manston, flying from Newcastle to Ostend and Stavanger for Lumb's Tours, and from Birmingham to Ostend for Hards Travel Service and JET Holidays. Manchester–Ostend tour services were also operated and the fleet of DC-4s carried pilgrims from many UK airports to Tarbes for visits to the shrine at Lourdes.

## LLOYD INTERNATIONAL AIRWAYS

Lloyd International Airways was founded on 18 January 1961 and initially used Douglas DC-4s to transport ships' crews to and from their vessels around the globe. However, insufficient work of this kind was found to keep the fleet busy and on 3 June 1961 Lloyd International also began operating inclusive tour flights. During the summer of 1962 the DC-4s carried holidaymakers from Gatwick to Palma and Perpignan, and from Glasgow to Ostend, Palma, Perpignan and Tarragona, principally on behalf of Mercury Air Holidays, a leading Scottish tour operator.

On 27 June 1964 a larger Douglas DC-6 entered service, flying from Glasgow to Barcelona on the first charter of a major contract for Mercury Air Holidays. This machine was in turn superseded in 1965 by a Bristol Britannia turboprop aircraft.

# CALEDONIAN AIRWAYS

Caledonian Airways (Prestwick) Ltd was established on 27 April 1961 by Adam Thomson (at the time a pilot with the charter airline Britavia) and John de la Haye, the New York-based North Atlantic manager for Cunard Eagle Airways.

Caledonian was to establish itself as a leading transatlantic charter airline, but also operated inclusive tour flights to the Mediterranean hotspots, initially using Douglas DC-7C four-engined airliners. Two of these were flown into the Biggin Hill Air Fair in May 1963, with one carrying invited travel trade guests on a special flight around the English south coast while the other remained on static display and was open for the public to view inside and out.

During the summer of 1963 Caledonian DC-7Cs operated inclusive tour services from Gatwick to Barcelona, Dubrovnik, Genoa, Malaga, Milan, Naples, Palma, Perpignan, Valencia, Venice and Zagreb, and from Manchester to Barcelona, Malaga, Palma and Valencia. In order to release the DC-7Cs for transatlantic charter work, two smaller Douglas DC-6Bs were leased from the Belgian airline, SABENA, for inclusive tour services during the summer of 1964, and one of these was open for the public to view at the 1964 Biggin Hill Air Fair.

# EURAVIA

One of Britain's most successful holiday charter airlines began life in a meeting on 1 December 1961 at the London office of Captain Ted Langton, the owner of tour operator Universal Sky Tours.

Captain Langton had founded Blue Cars in the 1930s to operate coach tours from the north of England to Devon and Cornwall. He had developed the 'hot bed' concept, whereby one group of holidaymakers departed a hotel at the end of their stay on the same coach which had just brought the next party, this method maximising bed utilisation and enabling him to achieve the very best hotel rates. He went on to apply the same principle when he moved into overseas coach holidays, and in the early 1950s he began paying large deposits to hoteliers in Majorca and the Costa Brava in order to secure guaranteed allocations of rooms, much to the annoyance of his competitors.

In 1953 he sold Blue Cars and launched Universal Sky Tours, offering package holidays by air to the Mediterranean resorts. However, the charter airlines of the time were unreliable and prone to sudden collapse as a result of their unsound financial resources. During 1961 alone two of the airlines he used, Falcon Airways and Air Safaris, had ceased operations. The resultant bad publicity reflected badly on his tour operation and caused him serious financial loss. As a result, he decided to set up his own in-house charter airline.

Also present at the meeting in London were aviation consultant J.E.D. Williams and Captain J.C. Harrington, and the result was the formation of Euravia (London) Ltd, with an initial share capital of £25,000. Derek Davison was also shortly to join the airline and be appointed chief pilot, and these gentlemen became its first directors.

The name Euravia was chosen because it seemed likely at the time that Britain would shortly join the European Common Market (now the EEC), and Captain Langton thought that if operations from a UK base were to prove impractical the same name could be used to launch services from a country such as Holland instead.

One of the first decisions to be made concerned the type of aircraft the new airline would use. During the winter of 1961–62 several possibilities were considered, including an approach made to Mr J.E.D. Williams by an aircraft dealer seeking to sell three Lockheed Constellation aircraft owned by the Israeli airline, El Al. These were inspected, and eventually a price of £90,000 was agreed for the three aircraft, fully overhauled and refitted in an eighty-two-seat configuration. Euravia now had to find a suitable operating base.

The management at Gatwick said that Euravia could use the airport as its base, but all aircraft handling and maintenance, passenger handling and catering must be contracted out to one of the established Gatwick operators. This was not acceptable, and so a meeting was arranged with Luton Corporation, the owners of Luton Airport.

The airport was, at that time, under used, with the only regular airline operation being an Autair scheduled service from Blackpool. It had a sound runway with reasonable navigational aids, and a newly built hangar was available. It was also close to the M1, making access easy from the Midlands as well as the London area. There were, however, no catering facilities and the tiny terminal building would not be able to accommodate even a single Constellation load.

Luton Corporation promised to have a new temporary terminal, capable of handling 250 passengers, ready within four months and it was agreed that Euravia would set up its operating base at Luton Airport. Part of the deal specified that the temporary terminal would not initially have a duty-free shop, thus leaving Euravia with a monopoly for its in-flight sales. An extension to the existing terminal was added during January–April 1962, and Euravia also set up its own London town terminal in a former tyre works near Euston Station, with passengers being coached between there and Luton Airport.

The Euravia base at Luton was opened on 1 April 1962 and the airline's first Constellation aircraft was delivered there on 12 April. On 17 April a welcoming party attended by the Mayor of Luton and other dignitaries was held in the Euravia hangar, which the airline initially shared with Vauxhall Motors, who used their section to store car bodies and components produced at their factory nearby.

The first Euravia route application put before the Air Transport Licensing Board was made in conjunction with Seamarks Bros Ltd (Airtours) of Luton, and was for:

> ... the carriage of inclusive tour passengers between Luton and Palma, the licence to be in effect from 26th May to 29th September 1962. The service to be operated at a frequency of one flight weekly in each direction with Constellation aircraft. The tariff to be from £53.11.0 to £72.19.6.

This application was granted, but only for a fortnightly frequency, not weekly. Euravia also secured a contract from a Midlands tour operator for the operation of its entire summer flight programme out of Birmingham. This fully utilised one Constellation, and the charter rate charged was 10 per cent higher than that charged to Universal Sky Tours.

The first Euravia commercial service took place on 5 May 1962, when a Constellation positioned empty from Luton to Manchester and then departed at 11.10 a.m. for Perpignan and Palma with Midland Air Tours clients. The air hostess on that inaugural flight was Marianne Allen, who was later to become the wife of J.E.D. Williams.

The aircraft arrived back at Luton just before midnight, and by then Euravia had operated its second service, an evening flight from Luton to Barcelona and Palma with seventy-seven Universal Sky Tours passengers. Commanded by Captain Don Tanton, the flight was not without its problems. En route to Barcelona in rain, its windscreen wipers stopped working. On arrival at Barcelona the wheel brakes jammed, and it was unable to take the Palma-bound passengers onwards. It was ferried empty back to Luton two days later.

A few weeks later all three Constellations were used to carry a large party of pilgrims from St Athan Airfield in Glamorgan to the shrine at Lourdes, and for the summer of 1962 they operated inclusive tour services from Birmingham, Luton and Manchester to Gerona, Malaga, Palma, Perpignan, Rimini and Valencia for Ellis Travel and Midland Air Tours, as well as carrying out the Universal Sky Tours flight programme.

In the autumn of 1962 Euravia was able to expand its fleet when it took over the struggling UK charter airline Skyways Ltd and its three Constellations. A deal was also struck with the receiver for the failed airline, Trans European Airways, for the lease of its two Constellations at the rate of £20 per flying hour. Euravia now had a fleet of eight Constellations.

They had been acquired at an attractively low price, but their operating costs soon proved to be high and they were not the most reliable of aircraft. They soon gained a reputation for oil leaks from their engines, and leaks in the fuel tanks and pressurisation system were also common. They were also prone to dripping hydraulic fluid onto the tarmac while parked, and because of this they were allocated their own parking stand at Manchester Airport.

Despite these handicaps the Constellations soldiered on for the time being. Less than 20,000 passengers were carried in 1962, but in 1963 this figure exceeded 50,000, with around thirty-five departures each week from Luton, Manchester, Glasgow, Liverpool, Newcastle and Birmingham to twelve overseas destinations. A full hot meal was served on all Euravia services, but the Constellations were slower than the Douglas DC-6Bs and DC-7Cs operated by competing airlines and were thus becoming unattractive to potential charterers. More modern aircraft would be needed for the coming summer seasons …

# 6

# INTO THE JET AGE

The 1960s saw the introduction onto holiday charter flights of jet- and turboprop-powered aircraft which offered a significant improvement in speed and comfort over their piston-engined predecessors. The turboprop engine was basically a jet engine which used its exhaust gases to turn a propeller. The aircraft that used this form of propulsion were not as fast as the pure jets, but they were very economical to operate and their cabins were quiet and vibration free.

Some charter airlines were able to afford brand new aircraft, but for those who could not there was a ready supply of relatively low-mileage examples which were being prematurely retired by major carriers such as BEA and BOAC.

## BRITISH UNITED AIRWAYS (BRITISH CALEDONIAN AIRWAYS)

On 26 May 1963 Britain's largest independent airline, British United Airways (BUA), inaugurated a twice-daily 'Silver Arrow' rail-air service between London and Paris in conjunction with the French state railway company, SNCF. The air segment between Gatwick and Le Touquet was operated by turboprop Viscount aircraft and the total journey took around five hours, with the lowest fare being £10 9s 0d return.

During the summer of 1963 the Viscounts were also utilised on inclusive tour services from Gatwick to Barcelona, Basel, Deauville, Lisbon, Milan, Munich, Nice, Palma, Rimini, Toulouse and Valencia. In 1967 BUA concluded a deal worth £1,114,000 with Horizon Holidays for a series of flights to nineteen holiday destinations. This was the airline's largest inclusive tour contract to date, and was followed by a further Horizon contract worth £1.2 million for the summer of 1968. During this season BUA also operated holiday flights to Europe and North Africa for Leroy Tours, Lord Bros Holidays, Mediterranean Villas, Global Holidays and Lyons Tours.

By the summer of 1969 many holiday charters from Gatwick were being operated by new BAC One-Eleven jets, which BUA had first introduced on its scheduled service network. The Viscounts, meanwhile, were still giving useful service on inclusive tour flights from Luton to Gerona and from Gatwick to Gerona, Munich, Rimini and Venice.

Between April and June 1969 BUA took delivery of five new 'stretched' BAC One-Eleven srs 500s, which had been ordered specifically for its inclusive tour network. Their success on this work led to three more examples being delivered in time for the summer 1970 season, which saw flights from Gatwick to Dubrovnik, Faro, Ljubljana, Pula, Tenerife and Zurich, and from Birmingham to Ibiza and Palma, added to the busy tour flight programme. However, BUA was in financial trouble, and on 30 November 1970 the company was taken over by Caledonian Airways. The merged airlines were initially known as Caledonian/BUA, but this was later to be changed to British Caledonian Airways Ltd.

Caledonian Airways had itself placed BAC One-Eleven srs 500s into service in early 1969, and during that summer three were operated on behalf of Blue Sky Holidays and Global Holidays from Gatwick, Manchester and Glasgow to Greece, Italy, North Africa, Portugal, Spain and Yugoslavia.

In January 1970, Caledonian announced its purchase of a 40 per cent share in Blue Cars, the parent company of Blue Sky Holidays, for £1.3 million. A fourth One-Eleven was delivered in March 1970, but Caledonian's turboprop Britannia aircraft were still used on occasional holiday charters from Gatwick to Gerona, Ibiza, Munich and Palma. The airline's Boeing 707 jets were usually operated on transatlantic charters, but that summer they too were pressed into service on holiday flights, from Gatwick to Palma and Tenerife, and from Manchester to Palma.

After the takeover of BUA had resulted in the formation of British Caledonian Airways, one of the BCAL One-Elevens was involved in an incident at Corfu Airport on 19 July 1972. The aircraft was taking off on a return leg to Gatwick with seventy-nine holidaymakers and six crew aboard when its acceleration was retarded after running through a pool of standing water on the runway. The One-Eleven overran the runway and came to rest in a lagoon.

The failure of Horizon Holidays in February 1974 resulted in the loss of contracts worth £1 million and left three aircraft temporarily without work. Despite this setback, the inclusive tour fleet was gradually built up and by 1975 BCAL also owned a chain of ten Spanish hotels and the tour operators, Blue Sky Holidays and Golden Lion Holidays.

↑ Dan-Air BAC One-Eleven G-ATPJ at Gatwick. (Via author)

↓ An early Britannia Airways Boeing 737 aircraft at Liverpool Airport on a tour service in May 1970. (Via author)

↑ A Cambrian Airways Viscount aircraft, used on inclusive tour services from Bristol and Cardiff. (Via author)

↓ Channel Airways Vickers Viscount G-AVNJ. (Via author)

↑ BKS Air Transport Trident 1E G-AVYC, used on weekend inclusive tour services. (Via Captain Arthur Whitlock)

↓ A Laker Airways Bristol Britannia aircraft at Liverpool Airport on a charter service in July 1968. (Via author)

↑ Britannia Airways Bristol Britannia
G-ANBB. (Via author)

↓ A Dan-Air Comet 4 in flight. (Via
author)

↑ An in-flight portrait of BKS Air Transport Bristol Britannia G-APLL. (Via author)

# The big holiday jet-together.

## Cambrian Air Holidays – direct from Cardiff and Bristol.

New Cambrian Air Holidays are here with just what you need. A sunshine holiday in Ibiza or Majorca; on the Costa Brava, Costa Blanca or Costa del Sol; or in Italy and Austria. Choose your favourite. You'll have a great time – our experience will see to that.

You see, Cambrian Air Holidays may be a new name, but it's a consortium of Cooks, Lunn-Poly and your own holiday airline – Cambrian. So you get more than just a good holiday: you get the greatest holiday value going.

**Easy go, easy come.**
Right from Cardiff or Bristol airport, you're on holiday. From the minute you step aboard your Cambrian BAC 1-11, the pampering begins. And it only stops after we've jetted you home again.

**The start of it all.**
We'd like to tell you more because we want us to jet together. So send now for the handsome 32-page colour brochure that tells you all. It's lavish. And it's free.

To: Cambrian Air Holidays, 9/11 The Hayes, Cardiff, CF1 2DQ.

I want to jet away from it all. Please send me your free colour brochure.

Name................................

Address............................
........................................

*Cut out the coupon or see your travel agent.*

35

# BKS

In November 1961, BKS Air Transport was obliged to appoint a receiver, but despite this the company was able to continue operating and in April 1964 its first Bristol Britannia turboprop entered service. The four-engined former BOAC aircraft had actually been purchased by the north-east-based tour operator, Airway Holidays, under an arrangement that allowed BKS to use it for Newcastle–Heathrow scheduled services during the week, before operating Airway Holiday inclusive tour flights to Barcelona, Palma and Rimini with it at weekends.

The finances of BKS Air Transport were boosted in June 1964 when the state airline BEA took a 30 per cent shareholding, and during the summer of 1965 the airline operated inclusive tour charters out of Newcastle and Teesside airports. These were mostly on behalf of Airway Holidays and the majority of them utilised Britannia equipment, although by then turboprop Vickers Viscounts had also joined the fleet. From September onwards 'winter sun' flights to Seville, Marrakesh and the Canary Islands were operated by Britannias and also Viscounts.

For the winter of 1967–68 skiers were catered for on Britannia charters from Heathrow to Munich, Salzburg, Turin and Zurich, operated for winter sports tour operators. The first such service departed Heathrow on 17 December 1967, and for the rest of the season three Britannia flights were needed for each Sunday operation, leaving Heathrow at twenty-minute intervals.

In February and April 1969 two Trident 1E jet airliners were delivered to BKS. As with the Britannias, the Tridents were used for both scheduled services and holiday charters, with the first inclusive tour flight operating from Newcastle to Palma for Airway Holidays on 9 April 1969. In May 1969 BKS began operating inclusive tour flights from Leeds Bradford Airport to Barcelona, Gerona, Ibiza, Palma and Rimini, using Viscounts on behalf of the tour operator Wallace Arnold.

The 1970 summer tour programme included Trident services from Newcastle to Alicante, Gerona, Ibiza, Palma and Rimini for Airway Holidays, to Dubrovnik for Sunway Holidays, and to Bergen for Visit Norway. There was also a Saturday Teesside–Palma flight for Wallace Arnold.

On 1 November 1970 BKS Air Transport changed its name to Northeast Airlines, having become wholly owned by BEA. By the summer of 1971, Northeast had added flights from Newcastle to Trieste for Airway Holidays and Sunway Holidays, and to Ostend for Airway Holidays, to its charter programme. Following the merger of the state airlines BEA and BOAC to form British Airways, from 1 September 1973 Northeast Airlines was fully absorbed and began trading as part of British Airways Regional.

## JERSEY AIRLINES

In late September 1962 the small UK carrier Jersey Airlines began operating inclusive tour flights on behalf of Lord Bros, using two twin-engined Handley Page Herald turboprop aircraft. This short-range type was normally used on the airline's busy network of scheduled services out of the Channel Islands, but the Lord Bros tour programme saw the two Heralds flying from Gatwick to Athens and Rhodes, and from Jersey to Tenerife and Marrakesh, on the first inclusive tour services to use this type of aircraft over such distances.

On 1 November, the Air Holdings Group merged its subsidiary, Jersey Airlines, with the northern division of Silver City Airways to form British United (CI) Airways.

## TRADAIR

On 1 February 1960 the Southend-based airline Tradair took delivery of its first turboprop equipment, two former Aer Lingus Vickers Viscounts. These were reconfigured internally to accommodate sixty passengers and commenced inclusive tour operations with a flight from Southend to Palma on 6 May 1960. Throughout the summer one aircraft was despatched to West Berlin to fly German holidaymakers to destinations such as Barcelona, Naples, Palma and Rimini on weekdays, but it returned to Southend at the end of each week and both Viscounts spent the weekends carrying British tourists to Naples and Pisa.

It soon became apparent, however, that there was insufficient work for both Viscounts, and one was leased to Kuwait Airways. The bulk of the summer's inclusive tour work was thus still operated by the elderly Viking fleet. For the summer of 1961 Viscount equipment was used on weekend holiday charters from Southend to Catania, Munich, Naples, Nice, Palma, Perpignan, Pisa, Rimini, Treviso and Zagreb, but Tradair no longer held any contracts for flights out of Germany.

The collapse of Overseas Aviation in August 1961 made the banks very reluctant to loan money to the independent airlines to tide them over the winter months, and on 2 November 1961 Barclays Bank appointed a receiver for Tradair. It was decided to allow the airline to continue trading for one year in the hope that it could be returned to profitability in that time, and both Viscounts were placed into storage.

For the summer of 1962 the fleet of Vikings carried out a programme of inclusive tour flights. The receiver found a buyer for one Viscount and arranged a lease for the other, but by the deadline of 2 November Tradair's debts had increased to almost £200,000. An agreement was reached with Channel Airways for the takeover of the airline from 31 December 1962, and Tradair's last commercial service was operated on the 18th of that month.

# CHANNEL AIRWAYS

The acquisition of the Tradair fleet provided Channel Airways with its first turboprop, the Viscount that had been out on lease, and for the summer of 1963 this was joined by another four-engined machine, a Douglas DC-4 purchased from the USA. Channel Airways managed to fit eighty-eight seats into this elderly piston-engined airliner, and was to go on to acquire a reputation for cramming the maximum number of seats into all the aircraft it operated. The DC-4 was mainly used on Southend–Ostend scheduled services, but from May 1963 it also appeared on some inclusive tour flights, taking up to three hours for the journey from Southend to Perpignan.

For the 1964 season an expanded fleet of Viscounts was used for flights on behalf of tour operators such as Tartan Arrow and Riviera Holidays, with the first service of the summer departing Southend for Valencia on 15 May. These Viscounts were mostly equipped with seventy-one seats, and during the spring of 1965 they were kept busy operating short trips to Beauvais (for Paris) and Rotterdam (for the Dutch bulb fields) from Birmingham, Bristol, Cork, Gatwick, Luton, Manchester and Newcastle. The summer season saw the fleet engaged on inclusive tour work from Manchester and Southend to Barcelona, Malaga, Munich, Palma and Rimini.

Most of the flights out of Manchester were allocated to one particular Viscount, an ex-Kuwait Airways aircraft, as this was the only version in the Channel Airways fleet which had the range to reach all of the Mediterranean resorts without refuelling. The other Viscounts usually had to call in at airports such as Southend or Bordeaux to top up their tanks.

At the beginning of 1965 new performance regulations had been imposed on Vickers Viking aircraft. These restricted the maximum permissible payload of a Viking landing at Southend to twenty-five passengers. This was clearly uneconomical, and so the type was retired by Channel after the last revenue service to Basel on 4 January 1965.

In 1966 Channel Airways purchased a fleet of eleven Viscounts from the US operator Continental Airlines for a total price of just under £3 million. These were the larger srs 812 model, and Channel was able to increase the seating capacity to eighty-two for its inclusive tour operations. In order to maximise its revenue from this type of work the airline set up its own tour-operating subsidiary, Mediterranean Holidays. The new Viscounts entered service with a night flight from Southend to Palma on 26 May 1966, and three days later a regular series of Southend–Tangier tour flights commenced.

At the beginning of May another turboprop type had joined the Channel Airways fleet, the twin-engined HS 748. These smaller aircraft were mainly engaged on short cross-Channel scheduled services, but they were also to appear on some inclusive tour services, carrying up to fifty-eight passengers between Southend and Barcelona, Bordeaux, Perpignan and Rimini, usually at night.

For the 1967 season Channel Airways secured a contract with Riviera Holidays, part of the Thomson Holiday Group. The summer 1967 Riviera brochure included an eight-day holiday at the Hotel Fontaine in Ostend, flying from Southend by Channel Airways Viscount for an inclusive price of £18 18s 0d in high season. The same brochure also offered a rather more complicated twelve-day holiday to Greece. Participants in this tour flew from Southend to Milan and were then transferred by coach to the port of Ancona. Here they joined a ship bound for Patras, from where they were transported by road to the Hotel Bakos in the resort of Loutraki. The total cost of the tour was £54 12s 0d. At the height of the 1967 season Channel's Viscounts were operating up to eleven services each week to Milan, up to seventeen to Basel and four to Maastricht.

On 14 June 1967 Channel Airways became a jet operator when its first BAC One-Eleven was delivered to Southend. This entered service on 26 June and was used for inclusive tour flights to Ibiza, Malaga, Palma and Tangier. Not content with one jet aircraft type, on 5 October 1967 the airline signed a contract for five HS Trident 1E three-engined airliners. In Channel service these were to be furnished with 139 seats, including a five abreast row in the forward section of the cabin which Channel would market as 'family seats'.

In order to carry this large passenger load the Tridents were to have higher operating weights and be fitted with extra emergency exits, uprated engines and strengthened floors. In Channel's publicity material and on the aircraft's tail fins they were described as 'Continental Golden Jets'. However, although five examples had been ordered the airline was in fact only to take delivery of two aircraft.

The first Trident commercial service took place on 1 June 1968. Throughout 1967 and 1968 Channel Airways expanded its inclusive tour flight programme, adding departures from regional airports such as Bristol and Cardiff, where Channel took over contracts with the local tour operator, Hourmont Travel, which had previously been awarded to the Cardiff-based airline Cambrian Airways. Viscounts were used for these services.

Since early 1968 Channel Airways had been experiencing problems with operating its One-Elevens out of Southend because of the restricted runway length available, and also because of complaints from local residents about jet noise. The decision was taken to transfer jet operations to Stansted Airport, and during the summer of 1968 the One-Elevens and Tridents were used on holiday charters from there to the Mediterranean and the Canary Islands, as well as on flights from East Midlands and Teesside airports for Mediterranean Holidays.

In April 1969 Channel Airways was awarded a £5 million contract from Lyons Tours which covered all of the operator's inclusive tour programme from 1970 until the end of 1972. In order to be able to fulfil this contract, Channel would need to acquire more jets. The finance was not available for new aircraft, so a fleet of former BEA and Olympic Airways Comet 4Bs was built up in time for the 1970 season. In the meantime, the airline once again operated springtime Viscount flights to Beauvais and Rotterdam for Clarksons Holidays, and in the summer of 1969 flew from many regional airports, including Edinburgh, to the Mediterranean, as well as serving Stansted.

On 26 January 1970 the first of the Comet 4Bs was delivered to Channel Airways at Stansted. The fleet was fitted out in a 109-seat configuration, and that summer the aircraft operated to the Mediterranean from Birmingham, Glasgow, Manchester, Newcastle and Stansted. The One-Elevens, meanwhile, flew out of Manchester to Basel, Gerona, Ibiza, Malaga, Milan, Rimini, Valencia and Venice. Although heavily committed to the Lyons Tours contract, the jet fleet also operated inclusive tour flights out of Bournemouth, East Midlands, and Teesside airports for Mediterranean Holidays and Trident Holidays (both now subsidiaries of Channel Airways).

In addition to maintaining the scheduled service network, the Viscounts were also employed on charter work which included a weekly flight from Birmingham to Ostend. All this work took its toll on the aircraft, and most of the jet fleet spent the winter of 1970–71 either in storage or undergoing overhaul, leaving Channel hard-pressed to carry out its Lyons Tours commitments with a single Comet.

The prospects for the future looked bright, however, as in September 1970 Channel Airways had won a contract from a consortium of three German tour operators for a series of charters in the summer of 1971. The contract covered over fifty flights each week from West Berlin to Greece, Italy, Romania, Tunisia and Yugoslavia, and was worth over £1.5 million to Channel. The flights commenced in March 1971, and almost fully utilised one Trident and a One-Eleven during the summer months.

However, back in the UK, the Channel Airways jet fleet was plagued with technical problems throughout the summer of 1971. A former Mexicana Comet 4 was purchased as a source of spare parts for the Comet 4B fleet, but the airline still found spares for the Tridents and Comets hard to obtain. One Trident sat engineless at Stansted, having donated its engines to keep the West Berlin-based aircraft operational.

Throughout the summer passengers sometimes experienced delays of eight hours or more, waiting to board an aircraft which had still to operate its previous service. Aircraft had to be subchartered from other airlines, and over just one weekend this cost Channel Airways £12,000. At one point during the August bank holiday the airline had 373 passengers waiting at Stansted for four delayed flights to Gerona, while 600 passengers were waiting at that airport for flights home.

At the end of the summer 1971 season the Tridents were sold to BEA and the following winter was a quiet time for the airline. The jets did little flying, and on

1 February 1972 a receiver was appointed for Channel Airways. All jet flying ceased on 15 February, but the Viscounts and other smaller types continued to operate scheduled services until 29 February, when all operations ceased and the fleet was put up for sale.

## CAMBRIAN AIRWAYS

Cambrian Airways was originally established in 1936 as Cambrian Air Services. When civil air transport restarted after the Second World War, Cambrian had the distinction of operating the first post-war flight by a UK independent airline when its Auster aircraft flew small items of cargo from Pengam Moors Airfield, near Cardiff, to Filton, near Bristol. When the new airport at Glamorgan (Rhoose) was opened to serve Cardiff, Cambrian transferred its operating base there and began operating regional scheduled services.

By 1962 the airline had progressed to Dakotas and turboprop Vickers Viscount aircraft. An association was formed with locally based Hourmont Holidays, and by 1964 Cambrian Viscounts were flying for Hourmont, from Bristol and Cardiff to Barcelona, Nice, Ostend, Rimini, Valencia, Venice and Zagreb, and from Exeter to Palma. All of these inclusive tour flights took place at weekends, as the Viscounts were fully engaged on scheduled services during the week. The Dakotas were also used on Sunday charters from Swansea to Ostend.

In November 1967 Cambrian Airways and BKS Air Transport became wholly owned subsidiaries of British Air Services, a company set up by BEA to operate UK regional scheduled services. This was to lead to both airlines being absorbed into the state airline in the years to come.

Cambrian's first BAC One-Eleven jet was delivered in December 1969, and the introduction into service of a small fleet of these aircraft in 1970 coincided with the formation of Cambrian Air Holidays, a company set up in conjunction with Thomas Cook and Lunn Poly to offer inclusive tour packages from Bristol and Cardiff.

For the summer of 1970 the Cambrian One-Elevens flew from Bristol and Cardiff to Alicante, Barcelona, Ibiza, Malaga, Palma and Venice, and also operated a similar programme from Liverpool. The Viscounts were used for weekly charters from Bristol and Cardiff to Ostend.

During 1972 one of the One-Elevens was based at Gatwick to operate inclusive tour flights on behalf of BEA Airtours. On 1 April 1972 Cambrian Airways came under the control of the newly formed British Airways Board, and on 1 September of that year the airline became part of the British Airways Regional Division.

← Court Line Aviation BAC One-Eleven G-AXMJ. (Andrew Read)

← Court Line Aviation BAC One-Eleven G-AZEB in the lilac version of the livery. (Homage to Court Line website)

← Autair BAC One-Eleven G-AWBL ready for take-off on another inclusive tour service. (Ralf Mantufel)

↑ A Britannia Airways Boeing 757. (Via author)

↓ Dan-Air Comet 4 G-APDG at Liverpool Airport in 1971. (Via author)

↑↓ A Channel Airways 'Golden Jet' BAC One-Eleven. (Via author)

↑ Dan-Air Boeing 727 G-BAEF at Manchester in 1980. (Via author)

↓ Dan-Air Comet 4C G-AYVS at Manchester Airport in 1980. (Via author)

↑ The cover of a British Eagle passenger information booklet, depicting one of their Bristol Britannia aircraft. (Via author)

↑ A Skyways of London luggage label for their coach-air services. (Skyways Coach-Air website)

1953 **DAN✈AIR** 1983

30 years experience

Dan-Air Services Ltd., Bilbao House, 36/38 New Broad St., London.    Benham

2312 1000 80171

# INVICTA
# INTERNATIONAL

Your attention is drawn to the conditions
of contract printed inside this ticket

## PASSENGER TICKET/BAGGAGE CHECK

**Issued by: INVICTA INTERNATIONAL AIRLINES LTD., MANSTON AIRPORT, KENT.**

INV/T/019P/171

← A Court
Line Aviation/
Clarkson Holidays
sticker issued to
commemorate an
inaugural Lockheed
TriStar tour service
out of Palma.
(Homage to Court
Line website)

↖↙ Air 2000
stickers depicting
their Boeing 757
and Airbus A320
aircraft. (Via
author)

## Passenger ticket and Baggage check

Issued by

C583432

**court line**

Luton Airport, Bedfordshire

For Conditions of Contract see page 2
and Important Notices on pages 3 & 4

↑ A Court Line Aviation charter ticket cover. (Via author)

# Airtours

## Flight Only Guide
2006

WIN 2
FREE
FLIGHTS
See page 7 for details.

Flights from
**£89** per person
See page 4 for details.

May - October 2006

→ The cover of the Airtours/MyTravel summer 2006 flight-only guide. (Via author)

← An advertisement for Air 2000's scheduled services. (Via author)

↓ The cover of a Laker Airways Skytrain ticket. (Via author)

**Passenger Ticket and Baggage Check**    833:4200:497:211

Issued by Laker Airways Limited, Gatwick Airport – London, Horley, Surrey.

Trade mark    SCHEDULED AIR SERVICE

# LAKER

IMPORTANT: Before travelling you should carefully examine this ticket particularly the Conditions and Notices contained herein.

→ An Aquila Airways luggage label. (Via Dave Thaxter)

→ An advertisement for the new Aquila Airways service to Santa Margherita. (Via Dave Thaxter)

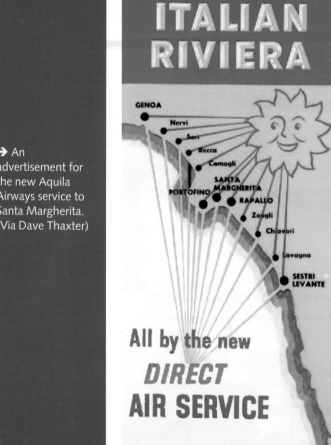

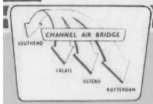

↑ British Caledonian BAC One-Eleven srs 500 G-AZMF at Liverpool Airport in 1972. (Via author)

↓ Monarch Airlines Boeing 737 G-DWHH at Manchester in September 1983. (Via author)

→ Britannia Airways Boeing 737 G-AXNB at Manchester in 1975. (Via author)

→ A Dan-Air Comet 4B on the stand at Manchester Airport in 1973. (Via author)

→ Laker Airways BAC One-Eleven G-AVBX at Manchester in 1979. (Via author)

→ Monarch Airlines Boeing 757 G-MONC at Manchester in 2000. (Via author)

## TREFFIELD INTERNATIONAL AIRWAYS

In late 1966 the small freight charter operator, Treffield Aviation, began a significant expansion when it secured a number of contracts for inclusive tour flights during the summer of 1970. The largest of these contracts was with Hourmont Holidays for flights out of Bristol and Cardiff airports and was valued at £500,000. Smaller contracts with other tour operators called for services from East Midlands, Gatwick and Liverpool airports.

The airline changed its name to Treffield International Airways in November 1966, and, as it owned no suitable aircraft for the services, arranged for the lease of three Viscounts from Channel Airways. The first one of these was delivered to Treffield's East Midlands Airport base in January 1967. The contracts called for the tour flights to commence in April 1967, but a delay in the award of Treffield's Air Operator's Certificate meant that for the first few weeks the services had to be subchartered to Channel Airways and British Midland Airways.

The problem was eventually resolved and Treffield began commercial operations in its own right during the last weekend of April, by which time a second leased Channel Airways Viscount had entered service. The Hourmont contract had placed the tour operator's entire flight programme out of Bristol and Cardiff in the hands of Treffield. The airline also had contracts to fly services out of Gatwick to Palma, Perpignan and Rimini for Sunair that summer, and it quickly ran into problems with providing sufficient capacity. The arrangement for a third leased Viscount from Channel Airways was cancelled, and in its place a larger Bristol Britannia turboprop aircraft was leased from Laker Airways, but this did not solve the problems.

A series of disputes between Treffield and Hourmont culminated in the announcement that Hourmont had cancelled the remainder of its contract with the airline. This, in turn, led to Treffield International Airways ceasing all operations on 23 June 1967, at the height of the holiday season. The contracts for the outstanding flights were taken over by a number of airlines, including Channel Airways, Cambrian Airways and Autair, and Treffield's directors presented their own winding-up petition. Lord Trefgarne, the airline's founder and managing director, attributed the failure to 'insufficient capital resources to ride out a very difficult business time'.

## INVICTA

After its 1968 programme of springtime bulb field flights ended, Manston-based Invicta Airways retired the last of its Vickers Vikings and acquired two turboprop Viscounts in time for the summer season. One was sent to West Berlin to operate flights for German tour operators and the other was employed on inclusive tour flights out of Birmingham, Manchester, Manston and Newcastle.

From October 1970 a small fleet of much larger Vickers Vanguard turboprops was built up, with two being used for passenger charters and others serving as freighters. The airline set up separate cargo and passenger divisions, with passenger operations being conducted under the name of Invicta International Airlines. The passenger Vanguards were mainly based at Luton, as Manston's remote location was considered unattractive to tour operators.

By the summer of 1972 the passenger Vanguard fleet had increased to four, and among Invicta's contracts was one from Tyrolean Travel for weekly flights to Munich from Edinburgh and Manchester. Pilgrimage charters to Tarbes were also operated from Blackpool, Cardiff, Gatwick, Luton and Teesside airports.

During the winter and spring of 1972–73 Invicta operated a series of day-trip charters from Bristol to Basel and Munich for shopping and sightseeing. These were well supported by the local population, but on 10 April 1973 one of the Vanguards on these services struck a mountain while approaching Basel in a snowstorm. Out of the 143 people aboard, 104 lost their lives. Despite this tragedy, a replacement Vanguard was obtained and the 1973 summer programme went ahead as scheduled.

Late in 1973 two Boeing 720B jets were added to the fleet. These were used on Invicta's own charter flights and also leased out to other airlines. Things did not go well, though, and during the summer of 1975 Invicta's owner, European Ferries, announced that the airline would cease flying at the end of October unless a buyer could be found. No suitable deal could be struck, and Invicta's last international passenger service took place on 21 October 1975 when pilgrims were flown back to Blackpool from Tarbes.

In December 1975 the airline's assets and goodwill were purchased by an aviation broking concern. The new Invicta resumed flying in January 1976, but this time as a cargo-only operator.

# BRITISH EAGLE INTERNATIONAL AIRWAYS

On 21 March 1960 it was announced that the Cunard Steamship Company had acquired a controlling interest in the Eagle group of companies which included Eagle Airways and Eagle Aviation, thus becoming the seventh major shipping line to diversify by taking a financial stake in a UK independent airline. By mid-May 1960 Cunard had completed the purchase of the entire share capital of the Eagle Group. On 28 July 1960 the airline was renamed Cunard Eagle Airways, but Harold Bamberg remained its managing director. Eagle had been operating flights out of Heathrow on a regular basis since 1957, and in anticipation of the closure of Blackbushe Airport the airline's operating base and engineering facilities had been transferred across in March 1960.

It was to Heathrow that the company's first Bristol Britannia turboprop was delivered on 24 March 1960, and in the years to come the airline was to build up a large fleet of these versatile airliners. A major setback occurred in June 1962, when Cunard formed an alliance with the state airline BOAC and the two companies set up a new airline called BOAC-Cunard to operate transatlantic scheduled services with Boeing 707 jets. This venture was to prove short-lived.

In the meantime, Cunard Eagle Airways remained in existence and on 14 February 1963 Eagle's founder, Harold Bamberg, bought back 60 per cent of Cunard's shares and regained a controlling interest in the airline. In September of that year the carrier was renamed British Eagle International Airlines, and in November the Liverpool-based airline, Starways, was taken over, along with its scheduled service network and a substantial number of contracts for inclusive tour flights out of Liverpool during the 1964 season. As the Starways fleet was not included in the takeover, British Eagle had to temporarily acquire Douglas DC-4s to carry out the tour services, disposing of them again at the end of the summer of 1964.

During that summer the turboprop Britannias were utilised on inclusive tour flights from Heathrow to Alghero, Barcelona, Basel, Biarritz, Lisbon, Naples, Nice, Palma, Perpignan, Rimini and Varna. Vickers Viscounts were also acquired, and in 1966 British Eagle took delivery of its first BAC One-Eleven jets. These entered service in May, initially on domestic trunk routes but later on scheduled services to holiday destinations such as Palma, Pisa and Rimini, and on holiday charters from Heathrow and Manchester on behalf of Lunn Poly, Everyman Holidays and Global Holidays.

In December 1966 Harold Bamberg and his associates purchased the remaining 40 per cent Cunard shareholding in the airline and regained full control. By the summer of 1968 British Eagle's inclusive tour programme was more extensive than ever, but the overseas holiday market was depressed by the economic situation at home, and the airline suffered extensive cancellations.

The One-Elevens flew from Liverpool to Ibiza, Palma and Rimini, from Birmingham to Ibiza and Palma, and from Manchester to Alicante, Gerona, Ibiza, Malaga, Palma, Rimini, Tenerife and Venice. Britannias operated three services each week to Gerona, and one was stationed in West Berlin throughout the summer to fly German holidaymakers to the Mediterranean. At the height of the season the airline's Boeing 707 aircraft, which had been acquired primarily to operate services to the Caribbean, were also pressed into service on Mediterranean tour flights.

# LAKER AIRWAYS

On 8 February 1966 Mr Freddie Laker, who had previously resigned as managing director of British United Airways, established his own charter airline, Laker Airways. He placed an order for three new BAC One-Eleven jets and immediately negotiated the lease of one of them to the Lord Bros tour company with effect from 28 April 1967. The lease covered the Lord Bros' summer 1967 inclusive tour and 1967–68 'air cruise' programmes, and was on a 'time charter' basis which placed the aircraft at the disposal of Lord Bros for a calendar year and guaranteed a minimum of 1,700 hours flying time.

While he was waiting for the One-Elevens to be constructed, Freddie Laker acquired two former BOAC turboprop Bristol Britannias in order to begin earning revenue. The first Britannia was handed over in March 1966 and the two aircraft were used that summer on ad hoc charters and on contract flying for other airlines, including Air France. Full commercial operations began in March 1967 with a series of inclusive tour flights from Gatwick and Manchester to the Mediterranean using One-Elevens and Britannias.

Tenerife was at the limit of the One-Eleven's fuel range, but Laker Airways was able to offer its clients non-stop flights there by limiting the number of passengers to seventy and restricting hold baggage to 40lb (18kg) per person. Tour operators were promised that as long as they adhered to these limits Laker Airways would cover any extra charges if adverse winds forced a refuelling stop at Lisbon.

During 1967 Freddie Laker bought out Arrowsmith Holidays, which had been operating tours from the north of England for over twenty years, and the following year he also acquired the Lord Bros travel company.

One-Elevens were introduced onto tour services out of Liverpool, and in February 1969 two former British Eagle Boeing 707s were added to the fleet. During the summer of 1969 these operated in 158-seat configuration on the longer inclusive tour flights to North Africa and the Canary Islands. Laker Airways was also able to secure contracts with German tour operators for holiday charters out of Berlin.

# BRITISH MIDLAND AIRWAYS

In 1970, British Midland Airways purchased two BAC One-Eleven jets specifically for inclusive tour work. These were operated out of Luton, Glasgow and Manchester to Alicante, Ibiza, Malaga and Palma for major tour operators of that time, including Clarksons Holidays, Vista Jet, Global Holidays and Horizon Holidays, and the airline's turboprop Viscounts were also utilised on a once-weekly Bristol–Palma charter operation.

When Court Line Aviation withdrew from operations out of Bristol in 1972 the contract passed to British Midland and its One-Elevens. However, the inclusive tour market was becoming very cut-throat at this time, and British Midland's venture into it was not a happy one. One jet was disposed of and the other one went on lease to Court Line Aviation for a time. British Midland then withdrew from the holiday charter market completely in order to concentrate on building up its scheduled service network.

## COURT LINE AVIATION

The colourful history of Court Line Aviation really began in April 1960 when a London-based helicopter operator called Autair Ltd branched out into fixed-wing aviation by acquiring a former BEA Dakota aircraft. By 1961 three Dakotas were in service on charter flights from a base at Luton Airport, and for the following summer season two Vickers Vikings were added to provide for further expansion into the holiday charter market. By the summer of 1964 three Airspeed Ambassadors were also in service, and these took over much of Autair's inclusive tour flight programme.

On 15 April 1965 it was announced that the entire share capital of Autair had been acquired for £215,000 by Court Line, the London-based shipping and shipbuilding group. From that time onward, much more effort was devoted to expanding the holiday charter operations of the airline, although its scheduled service network also continued to be served by turboprop aircraft for the time being.

During 1967 just over 97,000 passengers were carried on the tour flights, but by 1968 this figure had risen to 273,000, mainly due to the introduction of three BAC One-Eleven srs 400 jets. A total of 70 per cent of the capacity of these aircraft was contracted to Clarksons Holidays, which had been using Autair for the previous seven years.

On 31 July 1969 it was announced that Autair would be closing down its loss-making scheduled service network from 31 October in order to concentrate exclusively on inclusive tour charter work. In August 1969 one of the One-Elevens set a new world record when it logged a huge 402 hours and 36 minutes of flying time during that month. During the year the One-Eleven fleet was expanded to five, and over 500,000 inclusive tour passengers were carried.

On 11 September 1969 the airline's owners announced that from 1 January 1970 it would be renamed Court Line Aviation and would adopt a new, more colourful image. By then the airline had already negotiated contracts for the 1970 season with many leading tour operators, including Clarksons Holidays, Pontinental, Wallace Arnold, Mediterranean Villas, and the Midland Air Tour Operators consortium.

Seven new BAC One-Eleven srs 500s were delivered in late 1969 and early 1970. These were configured to carry 119 passengers on flights from Birmingham, Bristol, Cardiff and Luton to the Mediterranean. Each individual aircraft was sprayed in one of a variety of pastel colour schemes: pink/rose/magenta, or pale violet/mauve/ purple or light green/mid-green/forest green. The airline's vehicles were repainted to match, and tickets and stationery were also reprinted, with much emphasis on the airline's 'Halcyon' motif. A brochure produced for travel agents at the time described the new livery of the jets:

> They're painted in colours that we borrowed from sunsets and holiday beaches.
> Our aircraft are different on the outside. And different on the inside. Seats, walls and carpets all match the exterior colours. Remember how aircraft used to look inside? Grey. Ours don't, and it makes a pleasant change.

Female cabin staff were issued with new pinafore dress uniforms, designed to match the holiday atmosphere of the aircraft. One former Court Line air hostess recalled that her commencing salary at around this time was £708 per annum, on a seasonal basis, but with the possibility of permanent engagement at the end of the summer.

Court Line Aviation also pioneered the use of seat-back catering on its One-Eleven fleet. In place of the traditional tray service by the cabin crew, a cold meal was placed into a compartment in the back of each seat before the aircraft departed on its outward leg. A second meal was also loaded into each seat-back compartment, intended for the passengers on the return leg. Once airborne, the stewardess used a simple tool to release the first meal. However, many ingenious passengers found a way to use a coin to obtain the second meal as well, and spare portions had to be carried to compensate for this eventuality.

Court Line Aviation made a pre-tax profit of £431,000 in 1969, and on 26 May 1970 Court Line Aviation carried its 1 millionth passenger, on a Bristol–Alicante charter for Clarksons Holidays. By November 1971 the airline had twelve One-Eleven srs 500s in its fleet, allowing all but one of the original srs 400 models to be disposed of.

## BRITISH EUROPEAN AIRWAYS

Since the 1950s the UK state-owned airline, British European Airways (BEA), had been selling blocks of seats on its Spanish scheduled services to tour operators and travel agents, who were able to use special Inclusive Tour Excursion (ITX) fares to construct holiday packages.

On 1 April 1964, BEA launched its own tour-operating subsidiary, Silver Wing Holidays, and by 1966 the Silver Wing brochure was offering two weeks in Morocco for a package price of £84 12s 0d. By the end of the 1960s, however, BEA was losing serious amounts of traffic on its leisure-oriented routes to the charter airlines. The BEA fleet of Comet 4B jets was about to be retired and the decision was taken to use these aircraft as the initial equipment of a new charter airline subsidiary.

BEA Airtours was established on 24 April 1969, with a capital of £250,000 and a base at Gatwick Airport. The new airline was able to acquire hangar space at Gatwick that had recently been vacated by Transglobe Airways, and operations commenced on 6 March 1970 with a charter flight from Gatwick to Palma.

For the summer of 1970 BEA Airtours had nine former BEA Comet 4Bs in service. These were fitted out with 109 seats of the type used in the BEA mainline fleet of BAC One-Elevens, and the Comet's interiors were revamped by Charles Butler Associates, with the seat fabrics in blocks of royal blue, orange and yellow.

During the 1970 season the Comets operated out of Gatwick to Alicante, Gerona, Malaga, Nicosia, Palma, Pisa, Rimini, Tenerife, Trieste and Venice, and once weekly from Birmingham to Palma. More than 350,000 passengers were carried on 4,300 round trips, and the airline announced that it hoped to corner more than 20 per cent of the UK inclusive tour market by the following summer.

By late 1970 BEA Airtours was already looking at larger aircraft to replace the Comets, and in November of that year it announced that it would be purchasing seven Boeing 707 jets from American Airlines for £10.4 million. However, the airline's management came under fierce political pressure to obtain its new fleet from one of the UK state-owned airlines. This led to the cancellation of the arrangement with American Airlines, and in December 1971 BEA Airtours took delivery of the first of a number of former BOAC Boeing 707s. By the summer of 1972 two examples were in service on inclusive tour charters from Gatwick and Newcastle, but for the time being all of the Comets remained in operation.

As the Boeings were delivered, the Comet 4BS were gradually retired. By the summer of 1973 there were only five Comets operating alongside the Boeings, and on 31 October 1973 the last Comet 4B service arrived back at Gatwick at the conclusion of a charter to Paris for the NUS Travel Service. During their BEA Airtours service the Comets had carried 2 million passengers. Among the destinations served by the Boeing 707s from Gatwick were the Canary Islands, Morocco, Tunisia and Greece, and the type also operated fortnightly charters from Newcastle to Athens and Corfu.

The airline's parent company, BEA, also utilised aircraft such as Tridents, Vanguards and One-Elevens from its mainline fleet to operate off-peak inclusive tour charters from many regional airports, such as Exeter, Bristol, Cardiff and

Liverpool, to European and Mediterranean holiday destinations. In 1974, following the merger of BEA and BOAC into British Airways, the charter subsidiary also changed its name and became British Airtours.

For the summer of 1980, four Boeing 737 jets joined the fleet, but one of these was lost on 22 August 1985 when it caught fire and burned out with the loss of fifty-five lives during an aborted take-off from Manchester on a charter to Corfu.

## DAN-AIR

In 1966 Dan-Air signed a contract with BOAC for the purchase of two Comet 4 jets. After a lengthy conversion to a ninety-nine-seat configuration these aircraft entered service on inclusive tour flights during the winter of 1966–67 and became the first members of the large fleet of Comet 4s, 4Bs and 4Cs that Dan-Air was to build up and operate over the coming years.

During the summer of 1967 three Comet 4s amassed a total of 8,000 flying hours on Mediterranean inclusive tour flights for tour companies such as Clarksons Holidays and Horizon Holidays.

During 1968 the growth of the package tour industry was curtailed by government restrictions on the amount of foreign currency UK holidaymakers could take abroad with them, and by the economic situation generally, but Dan-Air was able to compensate for this by signing contracts with German tour operators such as Neckermann und Reisen for inclusive tour flights out of Berlin.

When the major UK carrier British Eagle International Airlines collapsed in November 1968 its charter flight contracts with Lunn Poly and Everyman Travel passed to Dan-Air. In order to fulfil these new obligations for the 1969 summer season Dan-Air needed to acquire more jets. Two more Comets were added, and two BAC One-Elevens were purchased from American Airlines. These required extensive modifications to meet UK airworthiness requirements and to refit them as eighty-nine-seat inclusive tour aircraft before entering service in the summer of 1969 on the Lunn Poly contract. This almost fully utilised the two One-Elevens, and as it called for some sixty flights each week out of Luton, Dan-Air established a base there, to which were attached twenty-three One-Eleven pilots, five Comet crews, fifty cabin crew and twelve engineers.

During 1969 Dan-Air carried 469,158 passengers on inclusive tour and other charters, and became the first airline to introduce disposable catering equipment on its aircraft. The 'Sky Diner' sets consisted of a larder made from special board and coated with metal foil to minimise fire risk, into which were fitted either eighteen or thirty-six meal/snack trays, also made from the special board. Dan-Air estimated that this equipment would save around £10,000 annually in cleaning costs and weight reductions.

For the 1970 season a fleet of eleven Comets and four One-Elevens was in use on inclusive tour services. The One-Elevens mainly operated out of Luton, while the Comets flew from Gatwick, Glasgow, Manchester, Teesside and Edinburgh to an extensive network of holiday destinations.

One of the Comets was, however, lost on 4 July 1970 when Dan-Air suffered its first fatal accident. A Comet 4 was on a Clarksons' charter from Manchester to Gerona and was approaching its destination when it struck a mountain and all aboard were killed. This tragedy occurred just two days after Dan-Air had announced a new four-year deal worth £2.5 million, covering the entire Global Holidays tour flight programme out of Birmingham for the summer of 1971. Under the contract, Dan-Air One-Elevens were to be used for flights to Alicante, Gerona, Ibiza, Mahon, Malaga, Palma, Tenerife and Venice.

In another deal for the same season, Dan-Air's Comets were to fly from Birmingham to Corfu, Faro, Ibiza, Malaga, Palma, Rhodes and Tenerife for the MATO travel consortium, and by the summer of 1971 Dan-Air was flying for almost all of the major UK tour operators. The longer range Comet 4Cs were in use in 119-seat configuration on routes to Las Palmas, Tenerife and the Greek islands, and even the airline's Boeing 707 jets, which had been acquired primarily for transatlantic charters, made an appearance on some of the more densely trafficked Mediterranean routes.

In 1972 Dan-Air began to search for a replacement for its fuel-thirsty Comets, and eventually decided to purchase three Boeing 727 jets from Japan Air Lines. These were ferried across the Pacific to the Boeing factory in Seattle where they underwent a major programme of modifications to qualify them for UK Certificates of Airworthiness. Boeing also revamped the passenger cabins to increase the seating capacity from 131 to 153 and installed extra emergency exits.

On 13 April 1973 Dan-Air operated the first Boeing 727 service by a UK airline, a charter from Manchester to Alicante. Two of the aircraft were also fitted with extra fuel tanks in their fuselages to enable them to operate non-stop from Berlin to Tenerife for German tour companies, and one example was stationed in Berlin for this work.

By 1974 Dan-Air had the most extensive inclusive tour flight network of any British airline, with departures from Aberdeen, Belfast, Bournemouth, Bristol, Cardiff, East Midlands, Gatwick, Glasgow, Luton, Manchester, Newcastle and Teesside, as well as Berlin. The collapse of Clarksons Holidays during that year did not affect Dan-Air too badly, as by then the airline's Clarksons contracts only accounted for about 11 per cent of its total business. Dan-Air was later to take over four of the BAC One-Eleven srs 500s of the failed Court Line Aviation, enabling more of the older Comets to be retired.

Before then, however, a Dan-Air Boeing 727 was to be involved in an unusual incident at Luton Airport. The aircraft was taking off for Corfu with 126 passengers and eight crew aboard when it took longer than usual to get airborne and struck some approach lights and instrument landing equipment sited beyond the end of the runway. Despite sustaining a 4ft gash in its hull and damage to its undercarriage the aircraft climbed away safely and the crew made an uneventful precautionary landing at Gatwick.

In June 1975 Dan-Air pilot Yvonne Sintes made UK aviation history when she commanded a One-Eleven charter from Gatwick to Heraklion as Britain's first female commercial jet captain.

Despite the introduction of their intended replacements, some Comets were still in service in 1976. One example was at the engineering base at Lasham undergoing engine runs after a lengthy technical problem on one particular day. In those days there were no engine mufflers at Lasham, just a 15ft earth bank to absorb some of the noise. After the engine runs had been completed Dan-Air received complaints that they had drowned out the funeral oration for Field Marshal Montgomery, who was being interred at nearby Alton.

The inclusive tour career of the Dan-Air Comets ended on 23 October 1979, when Comet 4B G-APYD landed back at Gatwick from Heraklion. However, there was to be one more chance for the public to fly in a Dan-Air Comet. On 9 November 1980 a special charter flight arranged by Ian Allan Ltd carried 119 Comet enthusiasts out of Gatwick on a local flight to the English South Coast and back, in the course of which low fly-pasts were made at former Comet haunts such as Heathrow, RAF Brize Norton and RAF Lyneham. On the same day as this last Comet flight was taking place, Dan-Air took delivery of its first Boeing 737. Over the coming years a mixed fleet of srs 200s, 300s and 400s was to be used on inclusive tour charters as well as scheduled services.

# BRITANNIA AIRWAYS

In 1964 Euravia signed a contract to purchase six stored Bristol Britannia srs 102 turboprops from BOAC. The total price of around £1 million included some specialised spare parts and was less than the purchase price of one Britannia srs 312 when new. As Britain still appeared to be many years away from joining the European Common Market, the name Euravia no longer seemed appropriate, so a new name was sought, and on 16 August 1964 the airline became Britannia Airways.

The first of the Britannia turboprops was delivered on 18 November 1964, and operations with the new type began on 6 December with a flight from Luton to Tenerife. The introduction of these aircraft enabled Britannia Airways to become the first UK holiday charter airline to serve its passengers hot meals – usually cottage pie!

During January and February 1965 two aircraft were converted to a new 112-seat layout, with the rest following suit over time. This standardisation allowed tour operators to provide a seating plan on their booking forms, from which passengers could request specific seats. The allocated seat numbers were then shown on their tickets.

On 26 April 1965 the Thomson organisation purchased Universal Sky Tours and its subsidiary Britannia Airways for £900,000. By the summer of 1965, five Britannia turboprops were in service, and by August of that year the last of the Constellations had been withdrawn. By then the airline was already thinking about jet aircraft to replace the Britannia turboprops.

In December 1965 Britannia Airways received a presentation on the BAC One-Eleven srs 500 jet. The Douglas DC-9 was also considered, but eventually the airline decided that the Boeing 737 was the best aircraft for its requirements. The UK Board of Trade brought pressure to bear on Britannia to buy British by insisting that any Boeing 737s purchased would be subject to 14 per cent import duty, but despite this the airline went ahead with an order for three of the srs 200 version of the aircraft in June 1966.

The first example arrived at Luton from Seattle, via Montreal and Goose Bay, Labrador, on 8 July 1968. It entered service in late July in a 117-seat configuration, making Britannia Airways the first airline in Europe to operate the srs 200 version, and only the second in Europe (after Lufthansa) to operate Boeing 737s. Britannia Airways was eventually to purchase thirty-one Boeing 737s of various models, with the last example being delivered in March 1983.

In the meantime, eight Bristol Britannias also remained in service, but on 1 September 1966, G-ANBB was lost in what was, at the time, the worst accident involving a British registered transport aircraft. The turboprop airliner left Luton just after dusk on a night service to Ljubljana, Yugoslavia, with 110 passengers on board. It was approaching its destination when it crashed into woods about a mile and a half from the airport. Only nineteen passengers and one crew member survived.

Despite this tragedy, Britannia Airways continued to expand its activities and during the 1968 summer season operated flights on behalf of Sky Tours (formerly Universal Sky Tours), Gaytours, Luxitours, Riviera Holidays, Horizon Holidays and Global Holidays. Several of these companies already were, or were later to become, part of the Thomson travel empire. In order to cope with the demand for flights that year, Britannia Airways was obliged to lease in additional Britannia turboprop aircraft from Laker Airways and BKS Air Transport.

By the summer of 1969 five Boeing 737s, in a new 124-seat layout, were in service, and at the end of that season the withdrawal of the remaining Britannia turboprops began. By late 1970 Britannia Airways was a wholly owned subsidiary of the Thomson organisation, whose other subsidiaries included Thomson Sky Tours and a number of other travel companies.

For the 1970 season, eight Boeing 737s and a reduced fleet of four Britannias were flying out of Luton and many regional airports to Alicante, Genoa, Gerona, Ibiza, Malaga, Malta, Munich, Naples, Palma and Rimini. The turboprop Britannias could also be seen at Birmingham, Edinburgh, Gatwick, Glasgow, Liverpool, Luton, Manchester, Newcastle and Teesside, operating weekly charter flights to Munich during the period of the Oberammergau Festival. However, on 29 December 1970 G-ANBL operated the last Britannia Airways service by this type, in a flight from Genoa back to Luton.

On 27 April 1971 Lord Thomson announced to guests at the official opening of the Hotel Atlantic in Puerto de la Cruz in Tenerife that Britannia Airways was the UK's second largest independent airline and that turnover that year was expected to exceed £11.5 million.

During the winter of 1973–74 Thomson holidays and Britannia Airways began to develop the winter short break market, and were offering four- or five-day trips to places such as Majorca for around £18 or £19.

However, in the political aftermath of the Arab–Israeli War of October 1973 the oil-producing countries imposed massive price increases and Britannia's fuel cost of around 15p per gallon quadrupled. Fuel surcharges had to be imposed on holiday prices and this, combined with the falling value of the pound and industrial unrest in the UK, caused inclusive tour bookings for the summer of 1974 to drop by around 20 per cent.

Britannia Airways managed to weather the storm by leasing out several aircraft to other airlines. Rival airline Court Line Aviation did not survive, however, and its collapse in August 1974 promoted Britannia Airways to the position of largest charter airline in the UK. By 1975, thirteen Boeing 737s were in service and the airline was looking at larger aircraft types to satisfy its expansion plans.

## MONARCH AIRLINES

Towards the end of 1966 two directors of British Eagle International Airlines, Don Peacock and Bill Hodges, began plans to set up an aircraft engineering and maintenance organisation to serve the needs of the independent airlines of the time. As a result, their new company, called Airline Engineering, was formed in January 1967.

They soon found out that the existing airlines could not offer sufficient capacity to serve the expanding inclusive tour market, and that Cosmos Tours in particular needed more seats for its 1968 summer programme. This led to talks with Cosmos and the formation of Monarch Airlines Ltd on 1 June 1967.

The new airline needed an operating base, and its founders looked at Gatwick and Stansted, before deciding upon Luton Airport which had adequate existing facilities for operations and maintenance and excellent road links to a catchment area of around 20 million people in London, the Midlands and the north of England. To make travel from London more convenient Monarch Airlines also opened its own town terminal in Tottenham Court Road.

For its initial aircraft fleet Monarch chose the Bristol Britannia turboprop, and the first two examples were delivered in February and April 1968. A proving flight to Rome took place on 15 March 1968, and at 9.30 a.m. on 5 April the company's first revenue service carried passengers from Luton to Madrid. During 1968 Monarch Airlines carried out over 90 per cent of the Cosmos flight programme, and by the end of the year 119,000 passengers had been transported.

By the end of 1969 the passenger total had grown to 250,000, carried on an expanded fleet of six 143-seat Britannias. Two more examples were acquired in 1970 and, as well as operating a busy inclusive tour programme, the Britannias were also utilised on short trips from Manchester to Beauvais (for Paris) and Rotterdam (for the Dutch bulb fields) for Clarksons Holidays.

By now, Monarch Airlines was looking at jet equipment to replace the ageing Britannias and in 1971 it took delivery of its first four-engined Boeing 720B jet. This was reconfigured to accommodate 170 passengers and operated Monarch's first jet service on 13 December 1971, flying from Luton to Tunis.

During the period 1971–74 the Britannias were phased out as more Boeing 720Bs joined the fleet, and at 8.40 p.m. on 9 October 1974 Britannia G-AOVT landed at Luton at the conclusion of the last commercial Britannia passenger service in Europe. This aircraft was later flown to the museum at Duxford, in Cambridgeshire, for static display in Monarch Airlines livery.

The collapse of Court Line Aviation in 1974 led to the leasing by Monarch of one of Court's former BAC One-Elevens in order to carry out inclusive tour contracts from Bristol Airport, and the growth of Cosmos Tours soon necessitated the leasing of a second example. By 1975 Monarch Airlines was carrying over 3 million passengers annually and employed over 600 staff.

During the 1970s, new operating bases at Birmingham, Bristol and East Midlands airports were established and the airline's continued expansion saw two more Boeing 720Bs joining the fleet. In 1979 Monarch's founders stepped down, handing over control to Alan J. Snudden, the former managing director of Dan-Air Services.

Early in 1980 an order was placed for two new Boeing 737 srs 200s, with an option on a third. The first of these entered service later that year, on inclusive tour services out of Berlin in a 130-seat layout. By then Monarch Airlines was operating to seventy-five destinations from the UK and a further seventeen from Berlin.

# 7

# VERTICAL INTEGRATION

As the package holiday market expanded it became increasingly important for the holiday charter airlines to forge financial links with the tour operators. Such an arrangement had benefits for both parties. By possessing a stake in an airline, or even owning it outright, the tour operator could secure a guaranteed supply of flight seats at a preferential rate for the summer season and could exert some influence over the scheduling of flights and the standard of cabin service. The airline, in turn, achieved a degree of financial security and the capital investment needed to modernise its fleet.

This process was known as 'vertical integration'. In some cases the process worked in reverse, with charter airlines setting up their own tour-operating subsidiaries, and there were also instances of major scheduled service airlines, such as BEA and British Caledonian Airways, forming their own inclusive tour charter subsidiaries. Among the earliest tour operator/charter airline pairings were those between Court Line Aviation and Clarksons Holidays, between the Thomson organisation and Britannia Airways, and between Cosmos Tours and Monarch Airlines.

## COURT LINE AVIATION AND CLARKSONS

In April 1973 Clarksons Holidays was on the verge of bankruptcy. Court Line Aviation relied on Clarksons as its major source of income and had recently invested in two Lockheed TriStar wide-bodied jets which were almost entirely allocated to Clarksons for the next five summers, so something had to be done. Court Line stepped in and purchased 85 per cent of the tour operator for a nominal £1.

By January 1974, however, Court Line Aviation still needed to find further work for its fleet during the coming summer. Holiday bookings had been badly hit by the economic situation in the UK and events overseas. The Horizon Holidays Group was in danger of collapse, so Court Line acquired that holiday operation as well. However, Court Line Aviation was itself in trouble, so two One-Eleven aircraft were leased out to other airlines, and the airline's TriStar operations were concentrated on Gatwick departures only.

Despite these measures, in June 1974 it was announced that unless further financing could be found immediately the whole Court Line group of companies would be faced with bankruptcy. In an effort to safeguard British jobs, the UK Government bought the group's shipbuilding assets for £16 million. At the time it was thought that this would enable the tour-operating and airline operations to continue trading until at least the end of the summer season, but it was to transpire that at least £25 million was needed to ensure this.

Operations continued normally until the evening of 15 August 1974, when Court Line Aviation and the tour companies suddenly ceased trading. The fleet of two TriStars and nine One-Elevens was grounded, with several aircraft being impounded. A total of 49,000 passengers were stranded overseas and a further 150,000 customers lost the holiday they had booked and paid for. However, Court Line had previously lodged a £3.3 million bond with the Association of British Travel Agents (ABTA), and this was used to bring home the stranded holidaymakers on the aircraft of Laker Airways, British Caledonian Airways and British Airways. At the time this was the worst airline failure in UK history.

## THOMSON AND BRITANNIA

By 1977 Britannia Airways had become the largest charter airline in the UK, carrying more than 7.5 million passengers annually from eighteen British airports. During the following year the parent Thomson Group acquired the Scandinavian tour operator, Fritidsresor, and its in-house airline, Blue Scandinavia, which was then rebranded as Britannia Nordic.

In 2000 the Thomson Travel Group, including Britannia Airways, was bought by Preussag AG (subsequently renamed TUI AG) of Hannover, Germany, for £1.8 million. In 2004 the Britannia Airways fleet began to receive new livery with the Thomson name along the aircraft fuselages. In 2007, following the takeover of its parent tour operator, First Choice Airways was integrated into the Thomson airline operation. At first the combined airline was known as Thomsonfly (after a failed Thomson low-cost airline operation), but from November 2008 the carrier became rebranded as Thomson Airways.

## COSMOS AND MONARCH AIRLINES

The major UK charter airlines and their parent tour operators were beginning to drift away from their previous high levels of interdependence by 1987, and

Monarch Airlines' managing director, Alan Snudden, was quoted as saying, 'Vertical Integration is no good if you get two separate losses.' When Monarch had commenced operations in 1968, 95 per cent of the airline's flying was for its parent Cosmos Tours, but by 1987 this figure was down to around 10 per cent, with the majority of the flying programme contracted to other tour companies.

Monarch Airlines was part of the Globus Gateway group of Swiss travel companies by 1994, and in that year 2.5 million passengers were carried. For the summer of 1998 Monarch had a fleet of twenty-one aircraft with a combined capacity of 5,460 seats and was the UK's third-largest charter airline. That winter, the 'Monarch Plus' service was made available to tour operators. This utilised Monarch's automated seat allocation system and offered passengers an enhanced in-flight experience which included upgraded catering and complimentary drinks and headsets.

## OTHER COLLABORATIONS, MERGERS AND TAKEOVERS

In December 1982 British Caledonian Airways and the Rank Travel Group set up a new joint venture subsidiary known as British Caledonian Charter Ltd (later shortened to BCA Charter). Inclusive tour charter operations commenced in March 1983, and during the period March–October 425,000 passengers were carried on flights to Faro, Las Palmas, Malaga and Tenerife. In mid-June 1985 British Caledonian Airways sold its chain of thirty Blue Sky Travel shops to Thomas Cook & Son for around £3 million, but for the time being retained its Blue Sky Holidays tour operation.

The tour operator Arrowsmith Holidays was purchased from the liquidator of Laker Airways for £250,000 in September 1985. This company, along with Blue Sky Holidays and Jetsave Holidays, then operated under the umbrella name of Caledonian Leisure. In October 1985 a new charter airline called Cal Air International was set up to replace BCA Charter, and initially used wide-bodied Douglas DC-10 jets.

British Caledonian continued with the disposal of its non-airline subsidiaries in December 1985 and Arrowsmith Holidays was sold off to villa specialist Owners Abroad for a nominal £1, and in the same month Jetsave Holidays was sold to the Greyhound Corporation in the USA. This was followed shortly afterwards by the sale of all of British Caledonian's Spanish hotel assets.

For the summer of 1987 the tour operator Wings used Cal Air for 30 per cent of its flight programme. However, the lack of smaller, narrow-bodied aircraft was restricting the airline's flexibility, and so in March 1989 the first of two Boeing 737 srs 400s was delivered. These were employed mainly on inclusive tour flights on behalf of Wings, Blue Sky Holidays and Owner Services Ltd.

↑ An Air 2000 Boeing 757 in flight. (Via author)

↓ An aerial view of five Airtours International MD-83 aircraft and staff at the airline's Manchester Airport base. (Via author)

↑ The sole BAC One-Eleven aircraft used by the short-lived Air Manchester. (Via author)

↓ BAC One-Eleven G-AXMU of Welsh charter airline Airways International Cymru. (Via author)

↑ Excalibur Airways Airbus A320
G-OEXC in flight. (Via author)

↓ Two of Air UK Leisure's Boeing 737
aircraft. (Via author)

↑ Air UK Leisure Boeing 737 G-UKLA in flight. (Via author)

↓ An aerial portrait of Air UK Leisure Boeing 737 G-UKLA. (Via author)

↑ A Leisure International Airways Boeing 767-300ER. (Via author)

↓ An apron scene depicting Caledonian Airways cabin staff in their tartan uniforms and a piper in front of the airline's Boeing 757 G-BPEC. (Via author)

↑ Caledonian
Airways Boeing
757 G-BPEB in
flight. (Via author)

In December 1987 British Airways took a substantial stake in the airline, and on 1 April 1988 set up a new subsidiary called Caledonian Airways to take over the charter activities of British Airtours and British Caledonian Airways. As a result, on 25 May 1988 the Rank Organisation became the sole owner of Cal Air. The airline was later renamed Novair, and inclusive tour services were operated from Gatwick, Birmingham, Glasgow, Manchester and Newcastle to destinations in Europe and North Africa, with a small fleet of Boeing 737s and Douglas DC-10s, but all operations ceased on 5 May 1990.

In the meantime, the new Caledonian Airways had commenced operations with a fleet of four Boeing 737 srs 200s, four wide-bodied TriStars and two Douglas DC-10s. The company's aircraft retained the basic BCAL livery including the golden lion tail logo, and in 1994 four 233-seat Boeing 757s were introduced. These were named after Scottish lochs and the flight attendants were fitted out with uniforms based on the Princess Mary tartan.

Despite introducing these innovations, British Airways took the decision to dispose of its charter subsidiary, and on 31 March 1995 it was sold to the tour operator Inspirations for £16.6 million. Three Airbus A320 aircraft joined the fleet for the summer of 1995, but in 1997 the airline changed hands again, being sold to the US travel conglomerate Carlson for £40 million. In 1998 Caledonian Airways was acquired by Thomas Cook & Son, and in September 1999 it was merged with another Thomas Cook acquisition, Flying Colours Airlines, to form JMC Airlines.

During the late 1970s the leading UK scheduled airline, Air UK, had diversified into inclusive tour operations, building up a small fleet of BAC One-Eleven jets for this purpose. Following a reshuffle in 1981 Air UK's inclusive tour division and its One-Eleven aircraft were sold to Peter Villa, who resurrected the name of British Island Airways (one of the airlines merged to form Air UK) for his new charter operation.

Air UK then concentrated on scheduled services until June 1987 when Air UK Leisure was formed as a joint venture by Air UK and seat broker Unijet to operate European inclusive tour flights with a fleet of Boeing 737 srs 200s. Services commenced on 30 April 1988, with flights from the new airline's Stansted base to Genoa and Rome, and on the following day services from Manchester to Rhodes and from East Midlands to Palma were inaugurated. On 7 October 1988, brand new 172-seat Boeing 737 srs 400s replaced the older jets, and a fleet of seven was built up.

By 1994 Viking International Air Chartering, which claimed to be Europe's largest charter seat broker, had become a major shareholder. On 1 April 1996 Air UK's 50 per cent stake in the airline was purchased by the Unijet Group, and

Air UK Leisure was merged into Leisure International Airways, which specialised in long-haul charters.

During the 1970s the tour operator Intasun had risen to prominence by specialising in cheap package holidays using off-peak flight times. Dan-Air had traditionally been the company's airline of choice, but as the decade drew to a close it found it harder to offer Intasun attractive seat rates using its ageing fleet of aircraft. Two of Dan-Air's executives approached Harry Goodman of Intasun with a proposal to set up a new in-house airline for him and to equip it with the latest fuel-efficient jets. As a result, on 18 July 1978 Air Europe was established as a partner in the Intasun Group, with Intasun agreeing to take one-third of its seat capacity, all on off-peak flight timings, in return for a shareholding.

Deposits were placed on three new Boeing 737s for delivery from April 1979, and operations commenced on 4 May 1979 when 130 passengers were carried from Gatwick to Palma. This made Air Europe the first UK charter airline to begin services since Freddie Laker had launched Laker Airways, thirteen years previously.

During its first summer season Air Europe flew to twenty-nine destinations from Gatwick, Manchester and Cardiff, and in 1980 the airline entered into a pioneering 'cross-leasing' arrangement with Air Florida, whereby Air Europe took on two Air Florida Boeing 737s for the summer, returning them, plus two of its own 737s, to the USA in time for Air Florida's busy winter season.

By the summer of 1981 Air Europe was flying to thirty destinations from the UK, for Intasun and for many other tour operators, including Clarksons, Global and Thomas Cook. Hot breakfasts were provided on all morning departures, and from 1983 onwards the airline was voted 'Charter Airline of the Year' by travel agents for four consecutive years.

On 6 April 1983 the larger Boeing 757 was introduced, initially on Gatwick–Faro flights. The summer of 1984 saw the airline's third-party work at its peak, with contracts held with over forty UK tour operators. However, during the winter of 1984–85 the airline suffered several setbacks.

Intasun contracted out around 20 per cent of its tour flight programme to British Airtours, and the tour industry as a whole had to cope with unfavourable currency exchange rates. As a result, three of Air Europe's Boeing 737s were disposed of, others were leased out, and eighty staff were made redundant. It was at this time that Air Europe's managing director, Errol Cossey, left to start a new charter airline. However, the company was still trading profitably, and by the summer of 1987 Intasun's parent, International Leisure Group (ILG), was taking 45 per cent of Air Europe's capacity and a fleet of six Boeing 737s and three Boeing 757s was in service.

In 1989 ILG formed the Airlines of Europe Group with the intention of building up a network of scheduled services across Europe by 1993, utilising a pool of aircraft which all the partner airlines could use according to their seasonal requirements. However, the 1991 Gulf War brought about a steep decline in passenger demand which was aggravated by rising fuel costs and interest rates.

This caused a financial crisis within the ILG Group. A Swiss financier who had invested heavily in ILG went into receivership and Air Europe was forced to suspend operations on 8 March 1991, by which time the airline was scheduling around 400 charter and scheduled service flights each week out of Gatwick alone. Despite Air Europe's collapse, some of its European partner airlines, such as Spain's Air Europa, were able to continue operating under new ownership.

Airtours began life as a small tour operator based in the north of England in 1978. The company grew steadily, using Dan-Air for the bulk of its charter seat requirements, but in October 1990 the Airtours Group formed its own in-house airline, which it named Airtours International and equipped with an initial fleet of McDonnell Douglas MD-83 jets based at Manchester Airport.

In early September 1993 the Airtours Group paid £20m for Cardiff based Aspro Travel and its in-house airline, Inter European Airways. This had been formed on 21 March 1986 with the backing of the Welsh Office and South Glamorgan County Council, and commenced flying on 18 May 1987 with two leased Boeing 737s. By the time the full summer 1987 programme had commenced four Boeing 737s were in service. Two years later Inter European was operating from seven UK regional airports to the Mediterranean, North Africa, Cyprus and Madeira.

The Inter European Airways operation was merged into Airtours International in November 1993, and Airtours International inherited a number of Airbus A320s and Boeing 757s to add to its MD-83s. By early 1994 the Inter European fleet had been fully absorbed. In 1994 the Airtours Group expanded into Europe with its acquisition of the Danish charter airline Premiair.

During the winter of 1994–95 Airtours International boosted the utilisation of its fleet by beginning day-trip flights to a number of popular tourist destinations in Europe. However, a mishap occurred on 27 April 1995 when the left undercarriage of one of the MD-83s collapsed as it was touching down at Manchester at the conclusion of a flight from Las Palmas. Fortunately there were only minor injuries among the 171 passengers and seven crew members aboard.

In the spring of 1996 the MD-83 fleet was withdrawn, and the airline then standardised on Airbus A320 and Boeing 757 aircraft for its short- and medium-haul services. By March 1997 the company had grown to the point where it had

1,450 employees. Following the renaming of the Airtours Group as the MyTravel Group on 8 February 2002, Airtours International and Premiair were rebranded as MyTravel Airways on 1 May 2002. A fleet of Airbus A320s and A321s and Douglas DC-10s was operated from twenty-two UK regional airports.

In June 2007 the MyTravel Group was merged into the Thomas Cook Group, and rebranding of its airline began in March 2008.

In 1986 the tour operator and villa hire specialist Owners Abroad was concerned about its lack of an in-house airline such as that possessed by its rivals, Thomson and ILG. This led to the company's involvement in the formation of the new airline, Air 2000, in which it initially took a 76 per cent stake.

The Boeing 757 was perceived as being ideal for the company's route network, as it was able to carry 231 passengers non-stop on sectors such as Glasgow–Corfu. Two Boeing 757s were acquired, and these commenced operations on 11 April 1987 from the airline's main base at Manchester. This airport had been chosen because it was less congested than the London area airfields, but even so Air 2000 still expected its aircraft to have accumulated delays in the region of one and a half hours after three round trips to the Mediterranean on a Saturday in peak season.

At that time 50 per cent of the airline's seat capacity was contracted to Owners Abroad, and passengers were provided with a high standard of cabin service and hot meals. In its first year of operation Air 2000 made a profit of over £3 million from inclusive tour flights operated from Manchester to twelve Mediterranean destinations, and in 1988 two more Boeing 757s joined the fleet. In mid-1992 four Airbus A320s were acquired to meet the demand from smaller tour operators for smaller aircraft. By 1995, 4.3 million passengers were being carried annually from sixteen UK airports, and Dublin departures were added during the following year.

Around 70 per cent of the flying was on behalf of Air 2000's new parent company, First Choice Holidays, but the airline also flew for over twenty-five other tour operators. By 1996 Air 2000 was the third-largest UK charter airline. In March 1997 the fleet comprised four Airbus A320s and thirteen Boeing 757s and around 1,200 staff were employed.

In June 1998 First Choice Holidays took over rival tour operator Unijet, and this led to the integration of Unijet's in-house airline, Leisure International Airways, into Air 2000 in time for the start of the winter 1998–99 season.

The airline was renamed First Choice Airways on 7 October 2003 and in July 2004 it became the UK launch customer for the Boeing 787 Dreamliner, with an order for six aircraft (later increased to eight), intended for delivery from 2009.

← An Airtours International MD-83 aircraft in flight. (Via author)

← A Flying Colours Airlines Boeing 757 in flight. (Via author)

← An Air UK Leisure Boeing 737 on turnaround. (Via author)

← JMC Airlines Boeing 757 G-JMCF at Manchester in September 2000. (Via author)

↑ Excel Airways Boeing 737-800 G-BDPB at Gatwick in September 2003. (Via author)

↓ Sabre Airways Boeing 727 G-BPND at Gatwick in 1997. (Via author)

↑↓ British Airtours Boeing 737 G-BGJG at Manchester in 1980. (Via author)

↑ Orion Airways Boeing 737 G-BGTV at Manchester in July 1981. (Via author)

↓ Flightline BAe 146 G-OLHB at Edinburgh in 1994. (Via author)

↑ BEA Airtours Comet 4B G-ARCP at Manchester in 1971. (Via author)

↓ An Airtours International Boeing 757 on final approach in 1999. (Via author)

→ Air Europe Boeing 737 G-BMSM at Manchester in 1980. (Via author)

→ Sabre Airways Boeing 727-200 G-BNNI on final approach in 1999. (Via author)

→ A Virgin Sun Airbus A320 at Manchester in 2000. (Via author)

In March 2007, First Choice Holidays agreed to a merger with the German travel company TUI, to create a new UK company, TUI Travel.

Orion Airways (not to be confused with the 1950s airline of the same name) was formed as a wholly owned subsidiary of Birmingham-based tour operator Horizon Travel on 28 November 1978. Operations with a fleet of four Boeing 737 srs 200s commenced on 1 April 1980. Much emphasis was placed on flights for passengers from the Midlands, with departures from Birmingham, East Midlands, Luton and Manchester airports to twenty-five holiday destinations, and the 1-million-passenger milestone was passed in September 1981.

During the period up to 1984 over 90 per cent of Horizon Travel's flight programme was operated by Orion Airways. By 1985, ten Boeing 737s were in service, but from March 1985 the airline began to phase out this type in favour of larger aircraft. Two 324-seat Airbus A300Bs were leased from Lufthansa for the summer 1987 season, but on 18 August 1988 it was announced that Horizon was to be taken over by the Thomson organisation. Orion Airways was merged into Britannia Airways in January 1989.

Airworld Aviation was formed in October 1993 by tour operators Sunworld and Ibero Travel to fill the gap in seat capacity created by the merger of Inter European Airways into Airtours International that year. The new airline commenced operations from its Manchester base on 29 April 1994, using two leased Airbus A320s flown on behalf of Sunworld, with its first revenue service being from Cardiff to Faro on 1 May 1994. A third A320 was added in April 1995, and based at Bristol, and during that year 434,000 passengers were carried.

In 1996, parent company Sunworld became part of the Thomas Cook Group. By 1997 Airworld Aviation was carrying the clients of thirty-three tour operators in addition to those of Thomas Cook, and on 8 April 1997 it became the first UK airline to take delivery of an Airbus A321 aircraft. In June 1998 Airworld was merged into Flying Colours Airlines, following the acquisition of the Flying Colours Leisure Group by Thomas Cook.

Flying Colours Airlines had been established by the Flying Colours Leisure Group in November 1995 to service its Club 18–30, Sunset Holidays and Priority Holidays brands, and had commenced operations on 6 March 1997 with a flight from Manchester to Lanzarote. The airline's initial fleet of leased Boeing 757s and Airbus

A320s was operated from bases at Manchester, Gatwick and Glasgow, to Spain and the Canary Islands. A novel feature of the airline's Boeing 757s was a drop-down in-flight entertainment system, the first on a UK holiday charter airline.

After the integration of the Carlson Leisure Group and the Thomas Cook Group, Flying Colours Airlines and Caledonian Airways were merged in October 1998, and this led to the formation on 1 September 1999 of a new airline called JMC Airlines, after the initials of John Mason Cook, the son of the founder of Thomas Cook & Son.

For the summer of 1999, a fleet of Boeing 757s, Airbus A320s and A321s was operated out of several UK airports, including new bases at Bristol and Cardiff, and new destinations in Italy, Malta, Cyprus and Turkey were added. By the summer of 2000 a fleet of Airbus A320s and Boeing 757s was operating to the Mediterranean and North Africa from nine UK airports.

All aviation activities were amalgamated under the name of JMC Airlines from 27 March 2000, and during its first season of operations the airline carried 5.75 million passengers, but also attracted adverse passenger reaction to its 28–29in seat pitch and its poor timekeeping record. From late 2002, as the Thomas Cook brand was more widely recognised than the JMC name, all airline operations began to be harmonised under the Thomas Cook name. On 31 March 2003, following the acquisition of the Thomas Cook Group by the German tour company C & N Touristic, the airline was rebranded and renamed as Thomas Cook Airlines UK.

## SMALLER CONCERNS

As well as these major affiliations, several smaller airlines were created by tour-operating companies, not always with successful outcomes. Ambassador Airways was set up in February 1992 by the Best Group, which until then had been a significant client of Britannia Airways. Operations commenced on 21 May 1993 with a service from Newcastle to Larnaca. The initial fleet of two Boeing 757s was later joined by a Boeing 737, operated on Ambassador's behalf by the leasing company Air Foyle.

For the summer of 1994 services were operated from Birmingham, Manchester and Newcastle, but Ambassador Airways abruptly ceased operations on 28 November 1994 and was placed into administration on the following day. Air Foyle immediately set up Sabre Airways to take over its contracts for 1995, using two former Dan-Air Boeing 727s, one of which was later fitted with engine 'hush kits' to enable it to meet the new noise regulations for night flights out of Gatwick and Manchester.

Two Boeing 737s, formerly operated by Ambassador Airways, were added to the fleet and by 1997 Sabre Airways was operating tour flights out of Birmingham, Gatwick, Luton, Manchester and Newcastle to Mediterranean resorts and the Canary Islands. During that summer, new Boeing 737 srs 800s were introduced to replace the ageing and noisy Boeing 727s.

In 1998 there was much speculation that Virgin Holidays would purchase Sabre Airways and use the airline to operate its inclusive tour flights under the name Virgin Sun, but this did not happen. However, in November 2000 the Libra Holidays Group took a 67 per cent stake (later increased) in the airline and changed its name to Excel Airways, and in March 2004 the Avion Group acquired 40.5 per cent of Excel Airways. Flights were operated mainly from Gatwick and Manchester to destinations such as Greece, Cyprus, Turkey, Spain and the Canary Islands.

On 30 October 2006 a management buyout resulted in a rebranding of the airline as XL Airways, and by 2007 the airline was flying to over forty destinations in Europe, Egypt and the Caribbean from thirteen UK airports. However, on 12 September 2008 the company entered administration with debts estimated at £205 million and ceased operations, stranding around 90,000 holidaymakers abroad. Some 63,000 or so of these were travelling as part of an ATOL-bonded package holiday and so were repatriated without further cost, but those who had booked seat-only arrangements direct with the airline had to travel home at their own expense.

Although the possible purchase of Sabre Airways by Virgin Holidays in 1998 was not to be, the tour operator went on to set up its own tour operation and charter airline under the name of Virgin Sun, with airline operations commencing on 1 May 1999 using a pair of leased Airbus A320s. Bases were established at Gatwick and Manchester, and the fleet grew to include two Airbus A320s and two A321s. Unfortunately, the airline ran up considerable losses and in March 2001 First Choice Holidays (the parent company of Air 2000) bought up the Virgin Sun tour operation and its airline arm was wound up.

Airways International Cymru was formed by the leading Welsh travel agency and tour operator, Red Dragon Travel, and commenced operations from its Cardiff Airport base in early 1984 with a single BAC One-Eleven aircraft. A second One-Eleven, leased from British Island Airways, joined it for the summer of 1984, and from 1985 Boeing 737 jets were operated.

At the end of the 1987 summer season one of these aircraft went out on lease to a US airline, but problems over the contract and non-payment of the lease instalments caused financial problems for Airways International Cymru. In an effort to overcome these, merger talks were held with Paramount Airways but these were not successful. Operations were suspended in January 1988 and the airline's aircraft were repossessed. A successor company, Amber Airways, was set up and began operations from Cardiff and Manchester in May 1988 with two Boeing 737s. However, at the end of November 1988 Amber Air was taken over by Paramount Airways.

Many charter airlines set up by tour operators never progressed beyond a single aircraft. Air Manchester was owned by Pennine Commercial Holdings and was a sister company of Sureway Holidays, whose summer 1982 flight programme was originally to have been operated by Laker Airways. Air Manchester was established in April 1982, using many former Laker Airways pilots and cabin crew. The airline was based, appropriately, at Manchester Airport, and was equipped with a newly 'hush-kitted' BAC One-Eleven aircraft. Technical assistance was provided by British Air Ferries.

The airline's first service operated to Ibiza on 3 June 1982 and carried just eight passengers. During the summer of 1982 services were operated to Alicante, Barcelona, Faro, Ibiza, Malaga, Nice and Palma, but in September 1982 British Air Ferries took over the inclusive tour flight contracts and repainted the One-Eleven in its own livery.

Janus Airways was formed by the Midlands-based tour operator Hards Travel in 1982, and used two Handley Page Herald turboprop aircraft to commence services on 2 January 1983. During the summer of 1984, inclusive tour flights were operated from Coventry and Lydd airports to Beauvais and Ostend as part of a series of continental touring holidays. Vickers Viscounts were also used, but Janus Airways ceased operations in 1986.

Palmair Flightline was formed by Bournemouth company, Bath Travel, in 1993 to safeguard its supply of flight seats after three airlines used by the company went out of business in 1990. A single BAe 146 jet was operated on Palmair's behalf by Southend-based Flightline on inclusive tour services from Bournemouth and Southampton, but the venture was short-lived and the contract was terminated in 1999 when larger capacity aircraft were required.

# 8

# 'SEAT-ONLY' OPERATIONS

From the mid-1970s many independent-minded holidaymakers no longer wanted to stay in large hotels on package arrangements, but preferred to seek out their own accommodation and even to invest in timeshare part-ownership of villas or apartments. To cater for this new trend, tour operators and charter airlines began to offer 'seat-only' booking facilities.

In 1975 Cosmos Tours was offering 'packages' to Greece for as little as £59. These included seats on charter flights and a throwaway voucher for very basic accommodation, usually in dormitory-style rooms with no private facilities, as a way of satisfying the regulations of the time. Cosmos called these packages 'cheapies'.

By 1986 government attitudes had become more liberal, and in July 1986 Monarch Airlines launched a programme of scheduled services to holiday destinations under the brand name 'Crown Service'. These services grew to encompass flights from Luton to Alicante, Gibraltar, Malaga, Minorca, Palma and Tenerife, and the air fare also included in-flight entertainment, a four-course meal with wine, and hot towels. To market these flights a subsidiary company called Monarch Air Travel was set up, and in September 1995 Monarch Airlines launched its 'Crown Advantage' loyalty programme under which passengers could accumulate points to be used for free flights in the future.

In May 1985 Britannia Airways inaugurated its own scheduled services, beginning on the Manchester–Palma route. Other services followed, from Manchester to Las Palmas, Malaga and Tenerife, and from Gatwick to the Canary Islands, but by 1994 Britannia had dropped its scheduled service network.

Air Europe began seat-only scheduled services in May 1985. Gatwick–Palma was the first route to be served, followed by Gatwick–Gibraltar from 1 November 1985. By 1990 the airline could boast 335 weekly scheduled departures to twenty-four European destinations. This number of flights was 50 per cent more than the number of its charter services.

The restrictions imposed by the Cyprus government on charter flights by foreign airlines resulted in the inauguration of scheduled services from Gatwick to Larnaca and Paphos by Air 2000 on 3 November 1993. Although the advent of the low-cost carriers such as easyJet and Ryanair to some extent eliminated the demand for seat-only services by the charter airlines, in the summer of 2006 MyTravel Airways was still operating scheduled services for its parent group from Gatwick, Manchester, Birmingham and Glasgow to Spain, Portugal and the Canary Islands.

⬆ Monarch Airlines Airbus A321 G-OZBF
at Manchester in 2002. (Via author)

↑ Monarch Airlines Airbus A320 G-MPCD
at Manchester in 1994. (Via author)

# 9

# The Long-haul Market

Once they had acquired aircraft with sufficient range, many of the UK charter airlines tapped into an additional source of income by operating long-haul holiday flights for the more affluent leisure traveller.

One of the earliest exponents was British Eagle International Airlines, whose fleet of turboprop Bristol Britannias had originally been designed for long-distance flights. On 10 March 1964 one of these aircraft departed London on a 'round-the-world' charter for the Sir Henry Lunn travel agency chain. Fifty-eight passengers were aboard the service, which routed via Cairo, Karachi, Delhi, Bangkok, Hong Kong, Tokyo, Honolulu, San Francisco, Las Vegas, New Orleans and New York, before arriving back in London on 5 April 1964 after a total airborne time of sixty-five hours and twenty-five minutes.

In the spring of 1966 a British Eagle Britannia operated another such tour which took in visits to Jerusalem, India, Thailand, Hong Kong, Japan, Honolulu, Mexico and the USA, and then during the winter of 1967–68 the Britannias were used to open an inclusive tour programme to Kenya for Lunn Poly, with prices starting at £150 for a two-week holiday.

By April 1968 the type had been displaced from long-haul work by Boeing 707 jets, which inaugurated fortnightly services from London to Bermuda and Nassau for Lunn Poly on 21 April 1968. Tour prices ranged from £109 2s 0d to Bermuda to £152 18s 0d travelling to Nassau, and included hotel accommodation, car hire, a 66lb (30kg) baggage allowance and a deluxe in-flight meal service with free rum cocktails and wine. As both destinations were within the sterling area the government's £50 limit on spending money taken abroad did not apply.

Dan-Air also used Boeing 707s to operate a series of twenty-one day around-the-world charters for German tour operators during the 1970s. One such trip in 1976 commenced in Munich and took in Teheran, Delhi, Rangoon, Bangkok, Hong Kong, Taipei, Tokyo, Fukuoka, Honolulu, Oakland, Niagara Falls and New York. On certain legs of the journey the stewardesses entered into the atmosphere of the stopover by adding unofficial touches to their uniforms such as Japanese-style jackets for the departure from Tokyo, and Hawaiian 'mumu' dresses for the visit to Honolulu. Unfortunately, on take-off from Honolulu the aircraft suffered a turbine failure in its No 3 engine and had to turn back. A Douglas DC-8 jet was hastily chartered to carry the passengers on to their next port of call at Oakland, California, where the crew and the now repaired Boeing 707 re-joined them for the remainder of their itinerary.

In 1970, Britannia Airways ventured into long-haul charters, rather surprisingly using Boeing 737 aircraft for weekly flights to Hong Kong, Colombo and Bangkok. In February 1971 the airline received the first of two leased Boeing 707s. Although acquired primarily for use on transatlantic work, they were also used during the summer of 1972 for fortnightly Thomson charters from Gatwick to Montego Bay.

After the Boeing 707s were disposed of, Britannia concentrated on short- and medium-haul flights for an extended period, but returned to long-haul operations in the 1990s once a fleet of Boeing 757s and 767s had been built up. In 1997 a programme of flights to the Maldives, India, South Africa, Australia, New Zealand, the USA, Canada, Mexico and the Caribbean was operated, and during that year a subsidiary called Britannia GmbH was set up to provide holiday flights from Germany for German tour operators. This commenced operations on 3 November 1997, initially using a single Boeing 767 for services to the Dominican Republic and other Caribbean destinations.

In 1969 the Court Line Group announced that it was to build two hotels in St Lucia as the first stage of its expansion into Caribbean holiday operations, and that one of these hotels would be the largest in the Caribbean area. On 1 January 1970 the group's airline, Autair, was renamed Court Line Aviation and in 1971 the Court Line Group purchased a 75 per cent stake in Leeward Islands Air Transport as part of its strategy to bring more American and UK tourists to its new Caribbean hotels.

In August 1972 Court Line Aviation signed a £19 million order for two wide-bodied Lockheed TriStars for use on both Caribbean and Mediterranean tour flights. The first of these entered service in April 1973, and by the summer of that year both examples were operational, being used initially on busy Mediterranean routes. The TriStars began long-haul work in November 1973, flying from Luton and Gatwick to St Lucia, via a technical stop in the Azores. For this route their passenger capacity was reduced to a more comfortable 350 seats. Like the airline's One-Eleven fleet, they were painted in striking two-tone pastel colour schemes, with one aircraft being basically orange and the other one pink. After the airline's collapse in 1974 a TriStar carried out its final service, bringing holidaymakers back into Luton from the Caribbean at 9.39 a.m. on 16 August 1974.

On 26 January 1973, BEA Airtours' Boeing 707 flight KT001 departed Gatwick on the airline's first round-the-world charter service. This routed via Teheran, Delhi, Colombo, Singapore, Bangkok, Hong Kong, Guam, Nandi, Auckland, Pago Pago, Honolulu, Mexico and Bermuda, and arrived back at Gatwick on 25 February.

← Monarch Airlines Boeing 720B G-BCBB. The airline used this type on tour services to the Caribbean. (Via author)

← A British Eagle Boeing 707 in flight. These aircraft were used on Lunn Poly tour flights to the Caribbean in the late 1960s. (Via author)

← British Eagle Boeing 707 Phoenix, used on inclusive tour flights to Bermuda and Nassau in the late 1960s. (Via author)

→ A Monarch Airlines Airbus A300-600R in flight. (Monarch Airlines)

→ A Court Line Aviation Lockheed TriStar, one of two used on inclusive tour flights to St Lucia. (Homage to Court Line website)

→ An aerial portrait of a Monarch Airlines Airbus A330. (Monarch Airlines)

The same crew remained with the aircraft for the whole trip, being joined at Hong Kong by additional flight crew members to assist with the long trans-Pacific legs.

Under the new identity of British Airtours, the airline continued to use Boeing 707s for long-haul charters for a while before disposing of them. After British Airways took over British Caledonian Airways in December 1987, British Airtours was superseded from 31 March 1998 by the newly formed charter arm, Caledonian Airways, which used wide-bodied TriStars and Douglas DC-10s for long-haul holiday charters. By 1997 Caledonian Airways was flying year-round to destinations such as Barbados, Kenya and Goa, and was also operating scheduled services on behalf of British Airways to San Juan, Nassau, Grand Cayman and Tampa.

Monarch Airlines first ventured into long-haul operations at the beginning of the 1980s, when leased Boeing 707s were used for holiday charters to destinations which included St Lucia. In the spring of 1999 the airline took delivery of two new wide-bodied Airbus A330 aircraft. These were operated in a two-class configuration and featured a 'Premium Cabin' offering extra legroom, upgraded meals and a multi-channel entertainment system, as well as priority check-in and baggage handling at airports. For the summer of 1999 this service was exclusive to Monarch A330s operating non-stop flights from Gatwick and Manchester to Orlando, Jamaica, Cuba, Las Vegas and the Dominican Republic. In 2005 Monarch introduced Boeing 767s on its long-haul holiday flights.

Not all long-haul ventures proved happy experiences for their airline operators. Excalibur Airways had commenced inclusive tour services in May 1992, using Airbus A320 aircraft for flights from Gatwick, Manchester and East Midlands airports to the Mediterranean and North Africa. By late 1995 the airline was in financial trouble and on 22 November 1995 it was announced that it was to be acquired by the Scottish tour operator, Globespan, with the intention of concentrating on long-haul services from 1996.

Plans were made to acquire two wide-bodied Douglas DC-10s in the spring of that year and a third in mid-summer. Gatwick–Orlando services were inaugurated on 4 May 1996. However, the first two proposed aircraft were not available in time and Excalibur had to subcharter DC-10s from other operators in order to carry out its flight programme to Florida and the Caribbean.

One of these aircraft was particularly prone to mechanical problems, resulting in many delays and adverse publicity for Excalibur. At Manchester, many passengers refused to board a flight scheduled to be operated by this aircraft because of safety concerns, and on 8 June 1996 Excalibur Flight 099 aborted take-off from Orlando because of smoke in the passenger cabin. Large numbers of its passengers subsequently refused to re-board this aircraft and demanded hotel accommodation and booking onto other services.

The adverse publicity and the loss of public confidence were contributory factors when Excalibur ceased operations on 26 June 1996 and went into liquidation.

During its three months of long-haul operations the airline had amassed losses of around £1 million.

Another UK holiday airline to diversify into long-distance charter flights was Bristol-based Paramount Airways, which had commenced operations to Malaga and Tenerife in 1987. During the winter of 1987–88 the airline's MD-83 jets were utilised for weekly inclusive tour services from Gatwick to Goa via two intermediate stops, one at Sharjah, but in the summer of 1989 Paramount Airways encountered difficulties and ceased operations completely at the end of the 1989 summer season.

In 1994 Airtours International acquired a wide-bodied Boeing 767ER with which it could operate non-stop flights to the USA and which was used for holiday charters to the Caribbean, Gambia and Australia. The airline also used smaller Boeing 757s on long-haul services, and one of these was involved in an incident on 1 January 1998 while operating a holiday charter to the Dominican Republic.

The aircraft was scheduled to land at Puerto Plaza Airport with 220 passengers and eight crew aboard. After two unsuccessful instrument landing approaches the crew attempted a low-level visual approach, during which the aircraft made contact with the ground short of the runway. Fortunately, the crew was able to carry out an overshoot and divert to Santo Domingo, where a safe landing was made.

During 1998 Airtours International was also operating to Grand Cayman, Barbados, Montego Bay, Antigua, St Kitts and Puerto Vallarta, using Boeing 767s. For the summer of 2000 Airtours International introduced Glasgow–Havana and Manchester–Fort Lauderdale charter services, and flights to Brazil followed in 2002.

In March 1997, Flying Colours Airlines formed Airline Management Ltd in conjunction with British Airways, and this company then took over the operation of the British Airways' DC-10 services out of Gatwick to Florida, the Caribbean and Mexico, from Caledonian Airways; this arrangement lasted until 2002.

During 2000, JMC Airlines used Douglas DC-10 aircraft for holiday flights to the Far East, including services to Bangkok and Phuket via a technical stop in Abu Dhabi.

Early in 1996 the seat broker Unijet, part owner of Air UK Leisure with Air UK, purchased two wide-bodied Boeing 767ER aircraft for use on long-haul charter services to Florida and the Caribbean. The aircraft were to be operated under the name of Leisure International Airways, but flown by Air UK crews on that airline's Air Operators Certificate. As Air UK was gradually absorbed into KLM, Unijet bought out Air UK's remaining 60 per cent shareholding in Air UK Leisure and integrated its services into Leisure International Airways. On 9 July 1998 the sale of Unijet to the First Choice Group for £110 million was completed. By the spring of 1999 Leisure International's operations had been absorbed into Air 2000.

# 10

# TRANSATLANTIC SERVICES

In the early 1960s many of the UK independent airlines began operating charter flights to the USA and Canada under the 'affinity group' charter rules, which permitted them to offer rates that were lower than the scheduled fares to passengers who were all members of a bona fide association with a common interest other than just cheap travel. However, widespread abuse of the regulations led to spot checks on eligibility at airports and the offloading of some passengers.

Eventually, the authorities bowed to the public demand for cheap fares and permitted the introduction of more flexible charter fares which could be booked by individual travellers, and the scheduled airlines such as BOAC, Pan American and TWA also slashed their fares.

## CALEDONIAN AIRWAYS

One of the pioneers of group charter flights from the UK to the USA was Caledonian Airways (Prestwick) Ltd, which was formed on 27 April 1961 by Adam Thomson (at that time a pilot with the UK airline, Britavia) and John de la Haye (at that time the New York-based North Atlantic manager of Cunard Eagle Airways). The founders had originally intended to call their new airline Scottish Airways, but discovered that this name was already registered to BEA.

Caledonian Airways (as it was generally known) began life with funding of £54,000, and much emphasis was placed upon its Scottish links when trying to attract group traffic. Its first aircraft was a Douglas DC-7C leased from the Belgian airline SABENA. This was delivered to Caledonian's base at Gatwick on 15 November 1961 and was fitted out with 104 seats. An initial aircrew complement of ten pilots, two navigators, four flight engineers and nine flight attendants was recruited, and to reinforce the airline's Scottish image the attendants' uniforms incorporated the Ancient Black Watch tartan motif.

By November 1961 Caledonian Airways had opened a ticket counter in the terminal building at Prestwick Airport and was describing itself as 'Scotland's Own

International Airline' in its publicity material. Although it was soon to become best known for its transatlantic operations, Caledonian's inaugural service was a charter flight from Barbados during the night of 29–30 November 1961 (appropriately enough, on St Andrew's Day).

Inbound charters from Africa were also operated, and in the course of one of these the airline's first aircraft and its passengers were tragically lost in a take-off accident at Doula. However, another DC-7C was quickly leased from SABENA and operations continued.

Caledonian's inaugural transatlantic charter carried ninety-nine members of the St Margaret's Guild of Scotland to New York on 21 December 1961 and charter services from Gatwick to Canada commenced during the summer of 1962. By its first anniversary Caledonian Airways had built up a fleet of four DC-7Cs.

A major landmark occurred on 13 August 1963, when Caledonian was awarded a Foreign Carrier Permit for the operation of a closed-group charter programme between the UK and the USA by US President John F. Kennedy, becoming the first non-US airline to be granted such a licence.

The airline traded heavily on its Scottish associations to attract inbound bookings from ethnic organisations in the USA, and prior to the start of the 1964 summer season sent a sales team to New York to push its 'fly Scottish' message. Similar effort was put into attracting groups from the UK and by the start of the season 116 westbound charters had been booked, seventy-five of these departing from Prestwick and the remainder from Gatwick.

In 1964 the airline acquired its first Bristol Britannia turboprop aircraft, and by the summer of 1965 three were in service. These gradually took over the transatlantic services from the DC-7Cs, and by summer 1967 an expanded fleet of eight was in operation. In January 1968 Caledonian's first Boeing 707 jet entered service on affinity group charters to the USA and Canada.

During 1970 four transatlantic charter airlines were accused of breaches of the affinity group tariff regulations by the US Civil Aeronautics Board. Caledonian was the only UK carrier named, but the airline discovered that the term 'affinity of interest', used in the regulations, could be taken to embrace blood ties with Britons living overseas. Many groups were organised to cater for eligible prospective passengers in this category, including the Anglo-Scottish–American Group and the Anglo-American Families Association. One of the largest of the bona fide associations was the Paisley Buddies, which sent groups from Glasgow to visit relatives in the USA, and this had an American counterpart in the form of the British American Club, based in California.

In the UK, Caledonian representatives visited eligible associations, advising them how to amend their constitutions in order to satisfy the affinity group rules. Once they had booked, Caledonian arranged for a piper to play them aboard their aircraft and the charter rates included complimentary meals, drinks and overnight bags. By 1970 the airline had become the dominant UK carrier in the affinity group charter business, carrying around 800,000 passengers that year.

As well as Gatwick and Prestwick, Caledonian also served many UK regional airports, and on 7 October 1971 one of the airline's Boeing 707s became the first one to land at Cardiff Airport when it flew in to operate a charter to New York.

By November 1973 the airline had merged with British United Airways to become British Caledonian Airways Ltd, and had been awarded a major contract by Jetsave, the UK's largest organiser of low-cost transatlantic flights. British Caledonian continued to win new charter business until the late 1970s, when a policy decision was taken to build up an extensive network of transatlantic scheduled services, and the charters were discontinued.

## BRITISH EAGLE

On 16 June 1960, Douglas DC-6A G-APOM operated the first of a programme of transatlantic charter flights for Cunard Eagle Airways, flying from London Airport to New York via Prestwick, Shannon, Gander and Montreal.

The DC-6As were later superseded on this work by Bristol Britannia turboprop aircraft, and on 25 March 1964 the US Civil Aeronautics Board granted a permit to British Eagle International Airlines (as the airline was then retitled) to operate regular charter flights between the UK and the USA. Only a limited number of flights were made that year, but during the summer of 1965 British Eagle Britannias operated seventy-eight charters from London to New York and Toronto. This number increased to 139 for the summer of 1966, with services from London to Toronto via Gander, from London to New York via Manchester, and from Belfast to Toronto via Shannon.

The last full season of transatlantic operations by the Britannias was in 1967 as, on 3 February 1968, British Eagle took delivery of a former Qantas Boeing 707 for this work. On 23 March 1968 this aircraft operated its first London–New York charter service and was soon to be joined by a second. Bookings were only accepted from groups and associations, and the price per passenger to the US East Coast ranged from £57 to £64 for a round trip, including a full meal service. By June 1968 British Eagle had accepted advance bookings to the USA with a total value of almost $2 million, but on 6 November 1968 the airline abruptly ceased operations.

## DAN-AIR

In October 1970 Dan-Air announced that it had been granted a five-year permit by the US authorities for transatlantic charter flights, and that these would be commencing on 5 April 1971. A new joint marketing venture called Dan-Air Intercontinental was set up by Dan-Air and CPS Aviation Services.

It was at first thought that second-hand Douglas DC-8 jets would be acquired, but in the event it was a former Pan American Airways Boeing 707 that inaugurated the transatlantic flights at the end of March 1971. This was joined by a second example in 1972 and, during that year and the next, these two jets operated many charter services out of Gatwick, Manchester and Prestwick to the USA and Canada.

In August 1973 Dan-Air signed a £1.7 million contract with CPS Jetsave for up to seven flights a week during 1974, transporting up to 54,000 passengers from Gatwick, Manchester and Prestwick to Calgary, Toronto and Vancouver. This was followed in the autumn of 1975 by a £4.7 million contract from International Weekend Inc., of Boston, for the carriage of over 50,000 passengers from Boston to Gatwick and return, between March and October 1976. However, in 1978 Dan-Air operated its last transatlantic service, and the Boeing 707s were disposed of.

## LAKER AIRWAYS

In 1969, Laker Airways acquired two former British Eagle Boeing 707s and was granted permits for charter operations to the USA from the UK and various other European countries. Transatlantic affinity group charters commenced in the spring of 1970, and these almost fully utilised the 707s that summer.

In an attempt to avoid the problems experienced by other charter airlines over the eligibility of their passengers, Laker Airways hired a lawyer to obtain sworn affidavits from its own passengers at check-in, but difficulties still arose on occasions. On 27 March 1971 thirty-eight passengers had to be offloaded from a Gatwick–New York flight before it could leave, and two months later another Laker service had to depart without forty-six of its passengers after a delay of three and a half hours caused by extra checks by officials. These problems caused the airline's founder to give much thought to devising a new type of service which would dispense with the need for all passengers to be members of a bona fide association and to purchase their tickets well in advance.

In 1971 Freddie Laker announced his proposals for a new 'walk-on' service which he called Skytrain. There would be no need for membership of a group or for advance booking: passengers could simply turn up at the airport with their passport, purchase a ticket at the desk and board the aircraft. The one-way fare would be £37.50 in the summer and £32.50 during the winter months. These rates would be about a quarter of the IATA scheduled fare. He stated his belief that Skytrain would generate new traffic, adding a further 2 million passengers to the 14 million currently crossing the Atlantic each year.

← Caledonian Airways (Prestwick) used Douglas DC-7C aircraft to inaugurate their group charter services to the USA in December 1961. One of the fleet is seen here at Gatwick. (Via author)

← A British Caledonian Airways Boeing 707 in flight. (Via author)

← Britannia Airways used Boeing 707s for transatlantic group charter flights between 1971 and 1973. G-AYSI is seen here at Luton Airport. (Via author)

↑ Laker Airways Skytrain Douglas DC-10 G-AZZC taxying in at Manchester in 1975. (Via author)

↓ Laker Airways Skytrain Douglas DC-10 G-BELO at Manchester in 1980. (Via author)

On 15 June 1971 he applied to the UK Department for Trade & Industry for a permit to operate a no-reservations service between Gatwick and New York, using Boeing 707s on a daily basis during the summer and with four flights a week in the winter. He immediately encountered opposition from both the UK and US licensing authorities. In Britain, the Air Transport Licensing Board refused permission, but this decision was overturned on appeal in February 1972. However, the permission for the service only remained in place until 30 March 1972, when the UK Government revoked Laker's licence and told him that he would have to reapply to the new Civil Aviation Authority (CAA) when it came into being two days later.

In early April 1972 he duly applied to the CAA, this time requesting eleven flights each week during the summer and seven weekly in the winter. Boeing 707s were to be used during the winter period, but for the summer months he proposed using 345-seat wide-bodied Douglas DC-10s. On 5 October 1972 the application was granted by the CAA with the proviso that Stansted Airport would be used as the London terminal instead of Gatwick. US approval still had to be secured, but Laker Airways immediately commenced work on the installation of check-in desks and other facilities at Stansted and placed an order for two DC-10s which arrived at Gatwick in November 1972.

Pending US approval for Skytrain, the DC-10s were utilised on Mediterranean inclusive tour services and were also shown off to the travel trade and media in a series of demonstration flights around the UK.

On 11 January 1973 the UK Government designated Laker Airways as an official transatlantic carrier, and on 1 April 1973 Advance Booking Charter (ABC) services across the Atlantic were authorised. These were intended to replace the problematic affinity group charters and allowed bookings to be made by individual passengers, although these bookings still had to be made two or three weeks in advance.

A Laker Airways DC-10 operated the first ABC flight a day later, and an expanded fleet of three was used on these services out of Gatwick, Manchester and Prestwick to Boston, Los Angeles, New York, Toronto, Vancouver and Winnipeg.

Finally, on 15 June 1977, President Carter gave US approval for Skytrain services to the USA, and with this the UK authorities relented and allowed Skytrain flights to use Gatwick Airport. On 26 September 1977 the first Skytrain service departed Gatwick for New York at 5.35 p.m. On board were 272 adult and child passengers and three infants, giving this first westbound flight a load factor of 70 per cent. The return leg was fully occupied.

Accompanying the passengers on the outbound leg was Freddie Laker, who had been much in evidence during the lead-up to the inaugural service. During the previous two days he had paid several visits to the Gatwick concourse, where he was warmly greeted by prospective Skytrain passengers, some of whom had begun queuing sixty-five hours in advance of departure. Similar queues were also reported in New York.

Once airborne, passengers could opt to consume food and drink they had brought aboard, or they could purchase an in-flight meal of paté, boeuf bourguignon, dessert, cheese and a small glass of wine for the sum of £1.75. In spite of the fact that a fall in the value of sterling had forced the London–New York fare up to £59 one way by the time of the inaugural service, Skytrain's first year of operation was a great success, with a reported profit of over £2 million.

Established competitors such as British Airways and Pan American Airways were forced to introduce their own 'no advance booking' fares on their services out of London, or lose traffic to Skytrain. Exactly a year after the first departure to New York, Skytrain flights to Los Angeles were added to the schedule, and on 3 June 1978 Freddie Laker received a knighthood.

In April 1979 Laker Airways ordered five more DC-10s, but on 25 May 1979 an American Airlines DC-10 crashed on take-off from Chicago, after one of its engines fell off a wing, and the US Federal Aviation Administration grounded all US-operated examples. DC-10s operated by British airlines were also grounded, but were allowed to return to service a few weeks later following structural inspections. By then, however, the groundings had cost Laker Airways £13 million.

During 1979 the CAA approved Laker's application to offer unrestricted tariffs in addition to walk-on fares on Skytrain services, and by 1980 fully pre-bookable super economy fares were available on all Skytrain flights. By 1981 Skytrain was operating from Gatwick to New York, Los Angeles, Miami and Tampa, from Manchester to New York, Los Angeles and Miami, and from Prestwick to Los Angeles and Miami. However, during that year aviation fuel prices soared and passenger numbers declined, and the many IATA airlines competing on the North Atlantic slashed their fares to attract custom.

Laker Airways was also suffering as a result of the unfavourable exchange rates. Its aircraft had to be paid for in US dollars, while its fares were calculated in sterling, and the pound was falling. The manufacturers of the DC-10 and its engines, McDonnell Douglas and General Electric, offered financial support amounting to £5 million but were forced to withdraw their offers when several IATA airlines threatened to boycott McDonnell Douglas products if the loans went ahead.

During the winter of 1981–82 Sir Freddie Laker attempted to diversify into the full-fare market by introducing a 'regency class' premium cabin on Skytrain services, but that season proved very costly to the airline, with many flights carrying very low passenger loads, although advance bookings for the coming summer season were encouraging.

The crisis came to a head on 4 February 1982, while Sir Freddie Laker was in New York filming a new Skytrain commercial. His bankers called in their loans, giving him until 5 p.m. that day to repay £5 million. He managed to get the deadline extended until 8 a.m. the following day, but was still unable to raise the funds and the banks appointed a receiver for Laker Airways. The airline collapsed early on the morning of 5 February 1982 with debts totalling £270 million.

Aircraft already in flight on services were recalled to Gatwick or Manchester, and thousands of passengers were stranded. During the following years Sir Freddie filed lawsuits under the US anti-trust laws against many national airlines, including British Airways, Pan American Airways, SABENA, Lufthansa and SAS, alleging conspiracy.

At that time, British Airways was in the run-up to privatisation. This would not have been able to proceed until the case was settled, and an adverse court decision would have had damaging effects on the company's flotation on the stock exchange. The damages awarded might also have bankrupted some of the other airlines cited, so, on 14 January 1985, the airlines being sued jointly offered Sir Freddie $50 million to end his court action. One week later he entered into a private settlement with British Airways. In July 1985 British Airways contributed almost $35 million to an out-of-court settlement fund to compensate Laker's creditors. The other transatlantic carriers involved also agreed out-of-court compensation payments and Laker's outstanding debts of $69 million were cleared.

## OTHER FORAYS INTO TRANSATLANTIC SERVICES

Lloyd International Airways acquired a Boeing 707 in April 1970 and used it for transatlantic affinity group charters out of Prestwick. A second example joined the airline in February 1971, and both machines were used for transatlantic flights out of Stansted and Prestwick. However, on 16 June 1972 Lloyd International ceased all flying and appointed a receiver.

In 1966 Transglobe Airways was awarded a US Foreign Carriers Permit for the operation of group charter flights between the UK and the USA, and operated seven such flights with Britannia turboprop aircraft during the last seven months of that year. During 1967 the Britannias operated twenty transatlantic sectors, including the first transatlantic passenger service direct from Birmingham to the USA on 16 July 1967, made possible by the lengthening of Birmingham's runway.

Then, in April 1967, Transglobe Airways signed a contract with the US carrier Seaboard World Airlines for the lease-purchase of six Canadair CL-44 turboprop aircraft, a 'stretched' derivative of the Bristol Britannia. These had been operated by Seaboard as freighters, but Transglobe intended to use them for low-cost transatlantic passenger charters. The first CL-44 arrived at Transglobe's Gatwick base in April 1968, and the inaugural service by the type was flight IK1226, which departed Gatwick for Niagara Falls with 170 passengers on 10 May 1968. At the height of the 1968 season three examples were operating charters out of

Gatwick, Belfast and Prestwick. A fourth machine was delivered late in 1968, but Transglobe found itself unable to compete successfully for contracts with rival airlines who were using DC-8 and Boeing 707 jets. On 28 November 1968 the airline suddenly ceased operations after two of its corporate creditors instituted winding-up proceedings.

Britannia Airways had a brief flirtation with transatlantic group charter operations in the early 1970s, receiving the first of two Boeing 707s on lease from US carrier, World Airways, in February 1971. However, the intense competition for transatlantic contracts drove down charter rates, and this and other problems led to a decision to dispose of the 707s in the spring of 1973.

Another airline which also encountered similar headaches with transatlantic charter work was British Midland Airways, which inaugurated services with a flight from East Midlands Airport to North America via Keflavík on 3 May 1970, using a Boeing 707. Unable to make money on the North Atlantic, British Midland withdrew from this market but was still able to use its 707s profitably by leasing them out to other airlines.

During the summer of 1989 Air 2000 was operating inclusive tour flights from Glasgow Airport to Orlando with Boeing 757s. Under the UK Government's Scottish Lowlands Airports Policy these services had to make a compulsory stopover at Prestwick Airport, only 24 miles into the journey, adding three hours to the trip time and adding £4,500 to the cost of each flight. This legislation had been introduced years before, at a time of lower traffic levels, in order to protect Prestwick's status as Scotland's only transatlantic gateway, but a judicial review ended this monopoly on 6 March 1990, and Air 2000 (and other transatlantic airlines) were henceforth permitted to operate transatlantic services direct from Glasgow.

During the period of April–November 1998 Airtours International leased a wide-bodied Boeing 747 from Air New Zealand and used it for services to destinations such as Sandford, Florida (for Orlando), in a 416-seat configuration. The aircraft operated out of Manchester six days a week and out of Cardiff on Fridays. A Boeing 767 was also leased from Air New Zealand for similar services out of Gatwick.

# 11

# NICHE OPERATORS

During the 1950s and 1960s many thousands of British holidaymakers were transported to their holiday destinations by a handful of specialised operators who had discovered their own unique ways of tapping into the market. These airlines were not reliant on contracts with inclusive tour companies, as they each provided scheduled services which could be booked individually by independent travellers. These operators were to enjoy great success in their own field, until changing circumstances and market trends brought about their eventual demise.

## AQUILA AIRWAYS

Aquila Airways was unique among UK independent airlines as its services were operated by flying boats, not land planes. The company was formed on 18 May 1948 by Wing Commander Barry T. Aikman DFC, formerly with 210 Flying Boat Squadron of the RAF. He initially purchased two former Hythe-class Short Sunderlands from the state airline BOAC, and after conversion these were put to profitable use on the Berlin Airlift, flying commodities such as salt and flour into Lake Havel on the outskirts of Berlin. The profits from this operation were used to build up a fleet of twelve Sunderlands and a single Short Sandringham, although only five of the Sunderlands and the Sandringham actually entered service, the others being used as a source of spare parts.

With the Berlin Airlift over, Aquila Airways had to find other work for its aircraft. A variety of ad hoc charters were operated and the company successfully applied for a BEA Associate Agreement for scheduled passenger services between Southampton Water and the Portuguese island of Madeira, which at that time did not possess a land airport.

On 24 March 1949 Short Sunderland G-AGEU *Hampshire* carried out a survey flight over the route, carrying a crew of eight, 100lb of Royal Mail and a party of invited guests. When it alighted on Funchal Bay, G-AGEU became the first commercial aircraft to visit Madeira. Scheduled services followed from 14 May 1949, on a weekly basis throughout the summer, with the aircraft also fitting in a round trip between Funchal and Lisbon before it set off back to Southampton.

In June 1949 Aquila Airways inaugurated holiday flights between Falmouth and the Isles of Scilly and during that summer the airline carried a total of almost 3,000 passengers. Plans were prepared for a series of luxury 'aerial cruises' around the Mediterranean in conjunction with the Thomas Cook travel agency, but there were insufficient advance bookings and the flights did not take place.

Aquila Airways commenced operations between Southampton and Jersey on 7 July 1950, with the aircraft alighting on St Aubin's Bay. This scheduled service was flown on Saturdays throughout the summer, with two round trips on each date, and was resumed for the summer of 1951.

Meanwhile, during the winter of 1950–51 Aquila Airways introduced the Short Solent flying boat into service. This type was considerably faster than the Sunderland and offered greater passenger comfort. The airline's first example was fitted out to accommodate forty-one passengers on two decks connected by a spiral staircase, and also featured a bar area.

For the summer of 1952 the Southampton–Madeira service was extended to serve Las Palmas in the Canary Islands. Two services were operated each week, departing Southampton at 12.45 a.m. on Wednesdays and Saturdays, the frequency being reduced to once weekly in the winter months. Solents operated this route, but the link between Funchal and Lisbon was still maintained by Sunderlands.

During 1953 two Aquila aircraft were lost in accidents, fortunately without fatalities, and in March 1953 the company was taken over by the British Aviation Services Group. No immediate major changes resulted, but this event was to lead to the eventual departure of Barry Aikman from the airline.

In 1953 the company was able to exploit a new source of revenue by operating a series of one-hour sightseeing flights from Southampton, carrying spectators over the large fleet of Royal Navy vessels formed up for inspection off Spithead by HM Queen Elizabeth II in her coronation year.

In March 1953, as part of a drive to convince the British public of the suitability of Madeira as a summer holiday destination as well as a winter one, Aquila Airways introduced a summer excursion fare of £59 10s 0d return from Southampton, valid for stays of up to twenty-one days' duration. This compared well with the winter fare of £89 2s 0d return. The hoteliers on Madeira also played their part by reducing their rates by up to 25 per cent for the summer season, in some cases offering accommodation for as little as 18s 9d per day. Aquila also offered the inducement of a 'money-back guarantee', whereby passengers would receive a full refund of the fare plus £40 towards hotel and other expenses if they experienced more than ½in of rainfall during a stay in July or August.

All of this promotional activity resulted in twice as many passengers travelling in May 1953 as had done the previous May, and Aquila carried a total of 6,000 passengers on its scheduled services that year. In order to minimise the effects of the ocean swell, services to Funchal were scheduled to depart Southampton Water at 11 p.m., landing just outside the harbour at Funchal at dawn, when the sea was at its calmest.

With an eye to future expansion the airline opened negotiations with the Ministry of Supply regarding the possible purchase of the three giant Saunders-Roe Princess flying boats that had been stored at Calshot since being rejected by their intended operator, the state airline BOAC, but the talks were fruitless and in the end Aquila acquired more Short Solents instead.

On 21 May 1954 Short Solent G-ANAJ *City of Funchal* operated a proving flight from Southampton to the Isle of Capri. On board this special service, which flew direct to the harbour at Gran Marina in six hours, were members of the press and a special guest, the well-known entertainer and Capri resident Gracie Fields.

When the scheduled service commenced on 3 June 1954 it became the first ever direct air link to Capri from the UK (previously, holidaymakers had been obliged to access the island via a ferry journey from Naples or Sorrento). The new service departed Southampton twice weekly at 3 a.m. and took eight hours and forty-five minutes for the journey, including a one-hour thirty-minute stop at the Marignane flying-boat base at Marseilles.

The flight was made at altitudes of between 7,000ft and 9,000ft, at an average ground speed of around 210mph. For most of the flight the passengers were free to wander around the two-deck interior of the Solent. The lower deck was divided into three passenger compartments, with toilets and ladies' and gentlemen's dressing rooms situated 'amidships'. The upper deck featured a bar area and a galley for preparing hot meals. The passengers were attended to by two stewards and two stewardesses, and the flight crew normally comprised two pilots, a navigator, a radio officer and an engineer. The service operated until September 1954, when it was suspended for the winter months.

In May 1955 the active fleet of Aquila Airways was at its peak, comprising three Solents, one Short Seaford and one Sunderland. On 4 June 1955 a once-weekly service to Santa Margherita, near Genoa, was inaugurated. This departed Southampton at 3 a.m. and reached its destination at 7.45 a.m., in time for breakfast ashore, and giving passengers the best part of an extra day on holiday.

On 8 January 1956, Solent G-AOBL was used to introduce a direct Southampton–Las Palmas service, but on 11 April its sister ship G-ANYI sustained damage to a float while alighting on rough water off Genoa. The passengers were swiftly ordered out onto the starboard wing to prevent the aircraft capsizing, and with the damaged float repaired the aircraft was back in service within forty-eight hours.

By this time, Aquila Airways was carrying more than 8,000 passengers annually and badly needed more capacity. It was found possible to increase the passenger accommodation in the Solents by replacing the cocktail bar and the ladies' powder room with more seats, and that year a new service to Montreux, on Lake Geneva, was added.

However, in July 1956 the last remaining Sunderland was retired, and on 26 September Solent G-ANAJ was wrecked when it was blown from its moorings at Santa Margherita and driven ashore during a gale at night. Aquila managed to acquire a replacement aircraft, and in 1957 operated flights from Southampton to Marseilles and onwards to Palermo and Corfu for the French tour operator Club Méditerranée, but by then the airline's operations were being run down.

On 15 November 1957 Solent G-AKNU *Sydney* left Southampton late at night, as flight AQ101 to Funchal and Las Palmas, with fifty-eight passengers and crew aboard. Twenty minutes later it crashed into a hill at Chessell Down on the Isle of Wight, with the loss of thirty-seven passengers and all eight crew members. It was later ascertained that both starboard engines had failed shortly after take-off, and the pilots were attempting to return to Southampton.

Aquila continued operations throughout the summer of 1958 with only three operational Solents, but the airline then announced that it would be closing down at the end of the season, attributing the causes to the lack of a suitable replacement for the ageing Solents and the increasing competition from landplane charter services to its destinations.

After a reception at the British Consulate in Funchal and a dinner party at the Miramar Hotel there, the final Aquila Airways passengers boarded a Funchal–Lisbon–Southampton service on 27 September 1958. A TV crew was waiting at Southampton to meet the flight, which was scheduled to arrive in daylight but was delayed by engine problems. It eventually arrived after sunset, the Solent flying its 'paying off' pennant as it taxied in. Its commander, Captain Weetman, was then interviewed under floodlights.

Aquila Airways officially ceased all operations on 30 September 1958, this date marking the end of all UK flying-boat services. The three surviving Solents were ferried to the Tagus Estuary near Lisbon, where it was hoped that a new Portuguese airline could be set up to operate them, but these plans fell through and the aircraft were eventually broken up there.

## SKYWAYS

In the early 1950s Eric Rylands, the managing director of the Lancashire Aircraft Corporation (LAC), pioneered the 'coach-air' concept by organising trips to the Isle of Man in which holidaymakers from all over the north of England were conveyed

↑ Two Silver City Airways Bristol Superfreighters loading at Ferryfield Airport. (Via author)

↓ A close-up view of the Bristol Superfreighter's nose-loading doors and the loading ramp used in the Silver City Airways car ferry operations at Ferryfield Airport. (Via author)

↑ Silver City
Airways car ferry
luggage labels.
(Via author)

↑ A British Air Ferries Aviation Traders Carvair gets airborne. (Via author)

↓ Passengers walk from their coach to the Skyways Coach-Air departure lounge at Lympne Airport. (Skyways Coach-Air website)

↑ The Skyways Coach-Air departure lounge at Lympne Airport. (Skyways Coach-Air website)

↓ The Skyways Coach-Air forward lounge at Lympne Airport. (Skyways Coach-Air website)

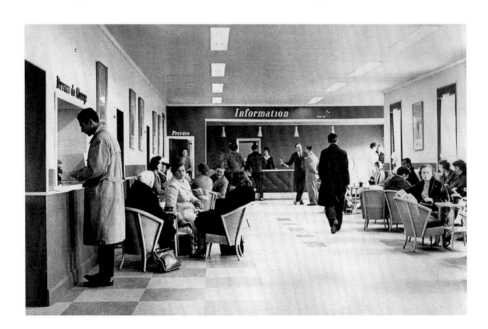

by coach to Blackpool Airport and transferred to the Rapide aircraft of LAC for the flight across the Irish Sea.

By 1954 he was managing director of Skyways Ltd as well as LAC, and applied to the Air Transport Advisory Council for a licence for a low-cost service between London and Paris using Skyways Dakotas for the air portion between Lympne Airport in Kent and Beauvais in France. The application was approved in 1955, and in July of that year it was announced that Skyways would be inaugurating a daily service in the autumn.

The airport at Lympne was acquired on a long-term lease, and on 26 September 1955 two Skyways Dakotas conveyed officials, dignitaries and journalists on an inaugural flight to Beauvais. Daily public services commenced at the end of that month, with thirty-two-seat maroon and cream coaches of the East Kent Road Car Co. transporting passengers from Victoria Coach Station in London to Lympne. After the fifty-minute flight the passengers boarded a coach of Transports Renault at Beauvais for the one-hour ride to the Hotel Moderne in Paris.

The initial off-peak fare was £7 14s 0d return (£1 more at peak times), compared to the BEA and Air France tourist-class fare of £15 9s 0d, and the service was an immediate success with 47,000 passengers being carried during its first year of operation. By the summer of 1956 three Dakotas were in use on the route and during that year Lympne Airport was purchased outright by Skyways, becoming the only privately operated, publicly licensed 'airport of entry' in Britain, complete with its own customs, immigration, health control and CID services.

During the first nine months of 1957 almost 30,000 passengers used the coach air service and at least sixteen round trips to Beauvais were operated each day in the summer months. A new route to Vichy was opened that year, and for the period of the Brussels International Exhibition in 1958 a twice-daily service between Lympne and Antwerp with coach connection to Brussels was operated.

In May 1958 more new routes, to Montpellier and Lyon (for Nice), were inaugurated. On 9 October 1958, following a group reorganisation, Eric Rylands formed a new company called Skyways Coach-Air Ltd to take over the services to Beauvais and Lyon, leaving Skyways Ltd still responsible for the Montpellier and Vichy flights. This service pattern was to remain largely unchanged throughout the next three years.

The summer of 1960 was a very wet one in south-east England. The grass runway at Lympne frequently became waterlogged, causing flights to be diverted to Gatwick, and during the autumn of that year the airport was closed completely for several days.

By 1961 an increase in passengers of almost 25 per cent had led to a requirement for larger aircraft, and in May 1961 the airline paid £750,000 for three brand new Avro 748 turboprops. A series of route-proving flights with an aircraft leased from the manufacturer commenced in November 1961, leading to the inauguration of scheduled services with the type on the Lympne–Beauvais route on 17 April 1962.

In September 1962 Skyways Ltd was taken over by Euravia (later to be renamed Britannia Airways), but Skyways Coach-Air was not affected and continued to operate normally as an independent company. By April 1963 three forty-four seat Avro 748s were in service. The passenger terminal at Lympne was enlarged to cope with anticipated further growth, and at the end of the summer season two Dakotas were converted to freighters, leaving just one in passenger service.

To raise public awareness of the coach air services, some of the Beauvais flights operated temporarily out of Biggin Hill Airfield during the period of the Biggin Hill Air Fair in 1963, and this exercise was repeated the following year.

For the summer of 1965 one of the Lympne–Beauvais services was extended to commence from and return to East Midlands Airport on a weekly basis. Things seemed to be going well for the airline, but during that year it suffered setbacks when well-publicised mishaps befell two of its aircraft.

In July, Avro 748 G-ARMX was operating Flight SX716 from Beauvais to Lympne. Arriving in bad weather conditions, it landed heavily on the grass runway, cartwheeled onto its back and skidded across the airfield upside down, coming to rest 200 yards from the control tower. The fuselage broke apart in the middle and the starboard wing was torn off, but there was no fire and no serious injuries were sustained. The aircraft was a write-off.

On 17 December 1965, Dakota G-AMWX was carrying twenty-nine passengers out of Beauvais and bound for Gatwick, as Lympne was out of action due to waterlogging. The Dakota suffered a massive electrical failure and the crew lost the use of all its radios and navigation equipment. They turned back for the French coast and had to make a forced landing in about 1m of water just offshore at Mers-les-Bains. All of the passengers were evacuated safely and bravely flew from Beauvais to Lympne in an Avro 748 the following day.

By 1967 the passenger fleet comprised four Avro 748s and the remaining Dakota. These were worked hard over the Easter holiday. On Good Friday the airport at Lympne stayed open around the clock and twenty-eight fully laden trips to Beauvais were completed, including two which had originated at East Midlands. Easter Monday was even busier, with twenty-nine Avro 748 and six Dakota round trips.

In order to raise finance in October 1967, 50 per cent of the company's shares were sold to the government-owned Transport Holding Company.

Accidents to Channel Airways' Avro 748s, while landing on the grass runways at Portsmouth Airport, convinced Skyways Coach-Air of the need for a hard runway at Lympne and a 1,350m concrete strip was laid there during the winter of 1967–68. This was first used when an Avro 748 landed at Lympne on 11 April 1968. Taxiways were added, Decca radar was installed and the construction of a new terminal building was put in hand.

On 9 May 1968 another Skyways Coach-Air aircraft suffered a mishap, again, fortunately without casualties. Avro 748 G-ASPL took off from Lympne for Beauvais but its nose wheel did not retract properly, becoming jammed at an angle. The aircraft was diverted to Manston Airport in Kent, which was a designated emergency airfield with extensive facilities. After flying around for two hours to burn off fuel the crew landed it safely on a carpet of foam laid on the Manston runway. The thirty passengers were evacuated safely and most of them later travelled to Paris on a direct flight from Heathrow. The aircraft was repaired and returned to service in due course.

Skyways Coach-Air retired its last passenger Dakota on 17 June 1968 after a service to Beauvais. During that year, a record 179,000 passengers travelled on the airline's scheduled services.

For 1969, six of the East Kent coaches were repainted in Skyways Coach-Air livery, and the airline introduced its 'Paristocrat' service on flights to Beauvais. For an optional fare supplement of £1, the upgraded passengers were treated to a buffet lunch and a choice of newspapers on the coach journey from Victoria Coach Station, and champagne and canapés on the aircraft.

On 10 June 1969 the new terminal building and office accommodation at Lympne were opened by the record-breaking aviator, Sheila Scott, who had arrived in her Piper Comanche aircraft, *Myth Two*, and the Leader of the Opposition, the Rt Hon. Edward Heath MP, unveiled a plaque to commemorate the renaming of the airfield as Ashford Airport.

At the peak of the 1969 summer season eleven flights were being operated each day from Ashford to Beauvais, with a further two staging through from East Midlands, and there were two flights each week from Ashford to Clermont-Ferrand and from Ashford to Montpellier.

Despite its apparent success, however, Skyways Coach-Air was in financial trouble. Since 1967 the Transport Holding Co. had loaned the airline over £1 million, and the balance sheet for the year up to October 1969 showed an accumulated deficit of £120,000. During the summer of 1970 the number of passengers originating in France declined considerably.

The routes to Lyon, Tours and Vichy were closed down, and in November 1970 a further loan of £300,000 was requested to sustain the airline through the winter months. Two instalments of £100,000 were received, but permission for the third instalment was withheld. As a result, on 20 January 1971 Skyways Coach-Air announced that it was unable to continue trading and operations ceased. Passengers holding tickets for travel within the next few days were re-booked onto other airlines and the others had their money refunded.

However, this was not quite the end of the story, for at the end of January 1971 a management buyout bid of £625,000 was successful. Included in the deal were four Avro 748s and ground handling equipment, but not Ashford Airport, although a temporary lease was taken out. The airline was renamed Skyways International, and services resumed on 8 February 1971 with 303 employees. However, the new company only lasted until 12 April 1972, when it was taken over by Dan-Air, as Dan-Air Skyways. Operations were transferred to Lydd Airport, but the coach-air services were then discontinued.

## SILVER CITY AIRWAYS AND CHANNEL AIR BRIDGE

In the 1950s the concept of aerial car ferry services was pioneered by Silver City Airways. The airline had been established on 25 November 1946 by a group of English and Australian industrialists in order to provide reliable air links between the UK and their overseas mining interests, particularly those in Australia. The airline acquired its title from the nickname of the mining settlement of Broken Hill, in New South Wales, a major centre for the Zinc Corporation's silver-mining operations.

Initially, Avro Lancastrian and Dakota aircraft were used for these services, but in October 1947 a Bristol 170 freighter was acquired on lease from the manufacturer. During the winter of 1947–48 the airline's managing director, Air Commodore Griffith Powell, experimented with loading cars into this aircraft, with a view to establishing car ferry services across the English Channel, enabling motorists to avoid the long queues at Dover and other ports.

On 15 June 1948 a proving flight between Lympne Airport in Kent and Le Touquet in France carried his Armstrong Siddeley Lancaster saloon car across the 47-mile route in just twenty minutes, and on 14 July 1948 the first commercial service was operated.

As Silver City was not at that stage licensed to operate such flights as a scheduled service they had to be organised on a charter basis, mainly in conjunction with the Automobile Association and the Royal Automobile Club, who promoted the flights to their members. A flood of bookings resulted, despite the fare of £27, one way, for a medium-sized car and up to four occupants being a good deal more expensive than the sea ferries. The service was operated successfully until it was suspended for the winter on 7 October 1948, by which time 174 cars and their occupants had been transported and the Bristol 170 fleet had been expanded to five aircraft.

The Lympne–Le Touquet service reopened on 13 April 1948, and on 2 May Silver City was granted a BEA Associate Agreement to operate the route on a scheduled service basis, for a one-year period. The initial frequency was three round trips per day, and the flights were operated in conjunction with Silver City's French associate company, SCAL.

By the middle of June bookings had been received for over 800 vehicles, and at the height of the season up to twelve daily round trips were being operated to cope with the demand. The busiest day of the summer was 28 July, when four aircraft completed twenty-three round trips and carried sixty-three cars. By the end of the season 2,600 cars, 7,900 accompanying passengers and 100 motorcycles had been transported and the car ferry operation had recorded a profit of £4,520.

For the summer of 1950 the loading and unloading of cars had been speeded up by the introduction of a new motorised loading ramp driven by a 2hp JAP (J.A. Prestwich Industries) engine. During that season an enterprising London taxi company was offering its customers a London–Paris taxi service utilising the Lympne–Le Touquet air link.

Two more Bristol 170s were acquired for the 1951 season and by the time the summer season commenced around 2,500 advance bookings had been taken. Early that year Silver City had been granted a further BEA Associate Agreement valid for five years and in November 1951 this was extended to ten years. As a result of this, the airline acquired the three Bristol 170s which had until then been operated by its French associate, Compagnie Air Transport, making 1952 a year of major expansion for Silver City.

On 10 January a new route linking Southampton and Cherbourg was inaugurated. Two aircraft were based at Southampton for this work, and until the car ferry traffic built up they were able to earn additional revenue by carrying consignments of cheese on the legs out of Cherbourg.

During 1952 Silver City placed an order for six of the new Bristol 170 Mk32 Superfreighter at a cost of £90,000 per machine. This development of the Bristol 170 featured a hold which was 5ft longer, capable of carrying three cars of any size plus up to twenty passengers. It also had more powerful engines and a new Decca navigation system which was especially suited to low-level cross-Channel operations. The new aircraft were to be delivered in the spring of 1953.

In the meantime, a new route between Southend and Ostend was inaugurated on 14 April 1952, but this was to last for just one season before the UK departure point was switched to Lympne. On 1 July 1952 Silver City completed its 10,000th Channel crossing without an accident.

The first of the new Superfreighters was delivered in 1953 and Silver City saw record-breaking Easter traffic levels, but the operations from Lympne were hampered by waterlogging of the grass surfaces there. In February, all services had to be temporarily transferred to other airports such as Southend. More heavy rain in September caused another temporary transfer of operations, this time to West Malling Airfield.

During 1952 Silver City had paid around £12,000 in landing fees to the Ministry of Civil Aviation, the owner of Lympne Airfield, and had persistently urged an improvement in the facilities there, but none had been forthcoming. As a result, the airline then announced that it intended to have its own purpose-built airport constructed at a site at Lydd, near Dungeness, and to operate it under the name of Ferryfield Airport. In the meantime, in June 1953 Silver City installed its own petrol pumps at Lympne so that its customers could top up their vehicle tanks to the permitted three-quarters full level before departure and thus save on the high cost of fuel on the continent.

Fares were reduced on the Lympne–Le Touquet services, and a new route was introduced from Lympne to Bembridge, on the Isle of Wight. The nine-minute crossing cost £3 for a small car and just 9s for accompanying passengers.

The construction of Silver City's new Ferryfield Airport was completed ahead of schedule and it opened to traffic with a special inaugural flight on 13 July 1954. Public services commenced on the following day and all schedules were then progressively transferred across from Lympne.

The final Silver City service out of Lympne departed for Le Touquet at 3.30 p.m. on 3 October 1954 and was fittingly operated by G-AGVC, the aircraft which had inaugurated the route in 1948. During its time at Lympne, Silver City had carried 54,600 cars, 18,372 motorcycles, 11,025 bicycles and 208,457 passengers on its services.

The new Ferryfield Airport cost £400,000 and came complete with two tarmac-covered runways, a large terminal building and apron space for six Superfreighters. With nine of these larger aircraft in service in 1954, the earlier Bristol 170s were then converted to all-passenger configuration and used on services to Ostend from that year.

On 7 April 1955 a new car ferry service across the Irish Sea was inaugurated. This linked Castle Kennedy Airfield, near Stranraer, with Newtownards in Northern Ireland, and took just twenty minutes for the crossing. From June 1955 an 'on request' service from Woodvale Airfield, near Southport, to Newtownards was added.

From 11 May 1956 the all-passenger Bristols were also used for the air component of a new 'Silver Arrow' coach-air-rail link between London and Paris. A coach conveyed passengers from Victoria Coach Station to Ferryfield, where they boarded a forty-four-seat Bristol 170 for the flight to Le Touquet. On arrival there, they boarded a coach for the short transfer to Étaples Station and a train into Paris, the whole trip taking some seven hours. A similar service also connected London and Brussels via Ostend. The same year also saw the introduction of car ferry services from Southampton to the Channel Islands.

For the 1957 season the car-ferry fares were reduced by between 6 per cent and 28 per cent and a three-tier tariff based on the date of travel was introduced. The cost of transporting a small car from Ferryfield to Calais or Le Touquet off-peak then became £6 10s, compared to £32 nine years earlier. At the end of the summer season the fares became even lower, enabling the owner of an Austin A35 car to fly it across the Channel for 4s less than the cost of the sea ferry. In 1957 the routes from Ferryfield to Calais and Le Touquet, from Southampton to the Channel Islands, and from Castle Kennedy to Newtownards were placed onto a year-round basis.

During the early and late months of 1959 the grass surfaces at Southampton also suffered problems with waterlogging and some services such as those to Cherbourg had to be transferred to Bournemouth Airport, which had the advantages of a hard runway and radar equipment.

At the beginning of 1960 Silver City signed a new route-pooling agreement with the French operator Cie Air Transport, and three of its Superfreighters were transferred across to this airline. By then, Silver City was beginning to experience financial difficulties. It sustained losses in 1960 and 1961 and its traffic figures were being affected by rival car ferry services, operated out of Southend to Ostend and Rotterdam, which had been inaugurated during 1955 and 1956 by Channel Air Bridge. It was becoming clear that Silver City did not have the resources to compete effectively with this airline, which had the financial backing of Air Holdings, the parent company of British United Airways.

Things became worse for Silver City on 1 November 1961 when the airline suffered its first fatal accident in 250,397 cross-Channel flights. Bristol Superfreighter G-ANWL overshot the runway at Guernsey while landing in poor visibility after a flight from Cherbourg and crashed 3 miles north of the airport. Both pilots were killed and seventeen passengers sustained injuries. On 23 January 1962 it was announced that Silver City Airways was to be taken over by Air Holdings and its operations merged with those of Channel Air Bridge.

From 25 February 1959 Channel Air Bridge had been the new name for the car ferry division of Air Charter Ltd, a small operator which had been acquired by aviation entrepreneur Freddie Laker in 1952.

On 14 April 1955 Air Charter launched car ferry services from Southend Airport, using Bristol Superfreighters on flights to Calais. In June 1957 the company began operating joint services to Ostend in conjunction with the Belgian airline SABENA, and during 1958 some 13,000 cars and 63,727 passengers travelled on its routes to Ostend, Calais and Rotterdam.

One requirement shared by both Channel Air Bridge and its rival Silver City was for a faster, more capacious replacement for the Bristol Superfreighter. Another of Freddie Laker's companies, Aviation Traders Engineering Ltd, devised a car ferry conversion of the cheaply available four-engined Douglas DC-4. This incorporated a new front fuselage section, with the flight deck relocated above a hinged nose door. Five cars and twenty passengers could be carried at 200mph over 250 nautical miles, and each conversion would cost £150,000.

Designated the ATL-98 Carvair (short for car-via-air), the first example made its maiden flight on 22 June 1961. By the summer of 1962 Channel Air Bridge had three in service, and the type was used to inaugurate car ferry services to Strasbourg on 1 June 1962. This was part of a network of 'deep-penetration' routes into Europe that was earmarked for the Carvair fleet, with the Superfreighters maintaining operations to closer destinations such as Calais, Rotterdam and Ostend.

By August 1962 Channel Air Bridge was carrying an average of eight cars and nineteen passengers on each round trip, and was having to turn away over twice as much traffic as it could carry. In October 1962 Channel Air Bridge was merged with the car ferry division of Silver City Airways, although for the time being they both continued to operate under their own names.

An accident on 28 December 1962 marred the end of a successful year for Channel Air Bridge. Carvair G-ARSF was approaching Rotterdam at the end of a flight from Southend when it struck a dyke 800ft short of the runway threshold, lost its starboard wing, and came to rest inverted. One of the pilots was killed, but the seventeen other occupants survived the crash.

On 1 January 1963 British United Air Ferries came into being and the car ferry operations of Silver City Airways and Channel Air Bridge were henceforth operated under this name. At this time, the car-ferry operations were at their peak. During the first two weeks of August 1963 the traffic exceeded all previous records.

The most spectacular growth was experienced on the 'deep-penetration' routes operated by the Carvairs to Basel, Geneva and Strasbourg, and during 1963 a new £150,000 car ferry terminal was constructed at Southend Airport. More new services followed in 1964, from Southend and Lydd (as Ferryfield was now renamed) to Liege, from Coventry to Calais, and from Bournemouth to Jersey.

By 1967, however, the competition from larger and more efficient 'roll-on, roll-off' sea ferries was making itself felt, and in February of that year the 'deep-penetration' routes to Basle and Geneva were suspended, along with other services from Manchester to Rotterdam and from Coventry to Calais. Many aircraft were withdrawn and placed into storage. On 31 March 1967 the last Superfreighter service from Southend was operated, although the type was still used on flights out of Lydd.

On 1 October 1967 a reorganisation within the group saw the car ferry operations split off from the rest of British United Airways and make a separate division within the Air Holdings Group under the new name of British Air Ferries. The car ferry services continued to be run down, with the last Lydd–Le Touquet Superfreighter service being operated by G-ANWM at the end of October 1970. Carvairs continued to operate out of Lydd to Le Touquet and Ostend until they too were withdrawn in early 1971.

On 27 October 1971 British Air Ferries was bought by Mr T.D. Keegan, who also owned Transmeridian Airways, a cargo operator using Canadair CL-44 turboprop freighter aircraft. Southend–Basel car ferry services were reactivated on 1 April 1972, initially using Carvairs, but on 13 May this type was superseded by the larger CL-44s. However, operational problems with the CL-44s resulted in their withdrawal and the return of the Carvairs on a thrice-weekly frequency.

By the summer of 1974 they were operating car ferry services from Southend to Rotterdam (three flights per day), Ostend (up to seven flights each day), Le Touquet (daily frequency), Basel (five flights per week) and Dusseldorf (twice weekly). By the summer of 1976, British Air Ferries had shifted its focus to all-passenger operations and had acquired Handley Page Herald passenger aircraft. The car ferry services were contributing less than 5 per cent of the airline's total revenue, and that year all car ferry operations ceased.

# THE SITUATION TODAY

Since the mid-1990s the emergence of the low-cost 'budget' airlines and the ability of holidaymakers to book their own accommodation online has significantly affected the traditional European package holiday and the need for dedicated charter operators. However, the major tour companies still maintain their own in-house airlines, operating long-haul flights to exotic destinations with the latest state-of-the-art equipment.

In 2002 Monarch Airlines rebranded its scheduled service operations as Monarch Scheduled. Six Boeing 787 Dreamliners were ordered in August 2006, but delivery delays and poor financial results in 2009 led to the cancellation of this order. In 2011 a £75 million cash injection was made by the airline's owners and the decision was taken to expand the scheduled service operations.

During the financial year to October 2012 Monarch carried 6 million passengers, of which less than 1 million were on charter flights. In 2014 Monarch had a fleet of thirty aircraft and offered some 7 million seats out of six UK bases. Long-haul destinations included Mexico, the Caribbean, the Gambia, Kenya, India and the Maldives.

On 31 March 2003 JMC Airlines was rebranded as Thomas Cook Airlines UK. In June 2007 a merger with MyTravel Airways created the UK's second-largest leisure airline. In 2014 Thomas Cook Airlines was expecting to carry some 6.7 million passengers to over fifty holiday destinations from eleven UK airports, using a fleet of thirty-five Airbus and Boeing aircraft.

In September 2007 the tour operators TUI and First Choice merged to form TUI Travel plc. Combined air operations of their in-house airlines commenced on 1 May 2008, with full amalgamation under the Thomson Airways brand being completed a year later. In May 2007 the TUI Group confirmed an order for eleven (later increased to fifteen) Boeing 787 Dreamliners. The first arrived in May 2013, and Thomson Airways became the first British airline to operate the type.

In 2014 Thomson Airways was flying from twenty-four UK airports to eighty destinations throughout Europe, the Mediterranean, the Caribbean, Mexico, North America, East Africa, India and Australia, with a fleet of fifty-five aircraft.

# The Low-cost Airlines

In 2014 the low-cost scene was dominated by the two great rivals, easyJet and Ryanair, both of which used as their model and inspiration the US budget carrier Southwest Airlines. However, over the years there have been several other low-cost airlines which have failed to stay the course.

In 1997 British Airways became concerned about the inroads being made into its short-haul traffic by easyJet and Ryanair, and initiated 'Operation Blue Sky' to examine ways of setting up its own low-cost services. Early in 1998 £25 million was invested in the creation of a budget airline subsidiary which came to be known as Go Fly and was based at Stansted Airport.

Go Fly's initial aircraft were three leased 148-seat Boeing 737s, and services were launched on 22 May 1998 with a flight to Rome. By early 1999 eight Boeing 737s were in service on routes from Stansted to Bologna, Milan, Venice, Copenhagen, Lisbon, Munich and Edinburgh, as well as Rome. Go Fly was not expected to break even for at least three years and made a loss of almost £20 million in its first year of operations, but succeeded in declaring a profit for the financial year ending iMarch 2001. By then, however, British Airways had decided that low-cost operations did not fit in with its future strategy, and it looked for a buyer for its subsidiary.

A management buyout secured Go Fly for a purchase price of £110 million in June 2001, and by early 2002 eighteen Boeing 737s were in service. However, in June 2002 easyJet purchased Go Fly for £374 million and gradually absorbed its operations into its own. The final service under the Go Fly name landed at Stansted just before midnight on 29 March 2003.

The low-cost carrier Buzz began life in a similar fashion to Go Fly, being established as a sub-brand of KLM UK, which was itself a subsidiary of the Dutch national airline. Buzz was initially equipped with eight BAe 146 aircraft transferred from KLM UK and based at Stansted. Services commenced on 4 January 2000 to seven destinations in Austria, France, Germany and Italy, and many of KLM UK's point-to-point domestic routes were also transferred across. Three months after opening reservations the airline had taken bookings totalling £100,000.

During the winter of 2000–01 flights were operated to Chambery and Geneva for winter sports enthusiasts, and for the summer of 2002 services were on offer to fifteen destinations in France alone. Boeing 737s were later acquired for the most heavily used routes, but in January 2003, after three loss-making years, Buzz was sold to Ryanair for £15.6 million. The airline was relaunched as Buzz Stansted and restarted operations on 28 April 2003 to a reduced network of twelve destinations from Stansted. After eighteen months, however, Ryanair decided to close down the operations and all flying under the Buzz name ceased on 31 October 2004.

On 10 January 2002 the UK scheduled airline bmi announced the creation of its own low-cost subsidiary to be called bmibaby. Operations commenced on 20 March 2002 with a service from the new airline's East Midlands Airport base to Malaga, and soon a fleet of Boeing 737s was in service on routes to Dublin, mainland Spain, the Balearics, Portugal, Prague and the south of France. Cardiff was added as a second base on 27 October 2002, and soon the airline's load factors were exceeding 74 per cent.

In its first year of operations, bmibaby carried over 3 million passengers and was voted 'Best Low-Cost Airline' in the *Daily Telegraph* Travel Awards. Further bases were established at Manchester and Teesside airports, and also at Birmingham, where three aircraft were based from January 2005. In 2009 the airline was serving over thirty European and UK destinations and was carrying around 4 million passengers annually in a fleet of over twenty Boeing 737s. However, following the sale of the parent company, bmi, to the International Airline Group (owners of British Airways), bmibaby was closed down and ceased operations in September 2012.

Flyglobespan was an offshoot of the long-established Scottish tour operator, Globespan, and was launched in November 2002. Operations commenced in April 2003 using two Boeing 737s chartered from the UK cargo airline Channel Express and based at Prestwick Airport. Low-cost services were operated from there to Barcelona, Malaga, Nice, Palma and Rome, with fares starting from £49 one way.

In later years the operating base was transferred from Prestwick to Glasgow Airport and an additional base was set up at Edinburgh. By the summer of 2006, Flyglobespan was serving fifteen European destinations and had introduced long-haul services to Florida using wide-bodied Boeing 767s. For the winter of 2006–07 low-cost services from Aberdeen and Liverpool to Tenerife were added.

By the summer of 2008 flights to sixteen European airports and five long-haul destinations were on offer from eight departure points in the UK and Ireland. Flyglobespan declared an operating profit of £1.2 million for the financial year 2008–09, but suddenly ceased operations and went into administration on 16 December 2009, leaving 4,500 passengers stranded.

One low-cost carrier that has stayed the course is Jet2, which was set up in October 2002 by the Dart Group, the parent organisation of cargo airline,

Channel Express, to provide low-cost passenger services from a base at Leeds Bradford Airport. The new airline's initial fleet was two Boeing 737s, and its first route, to Amsterdam on a twice-daily basis, commenced on 12 February 2003.

Over the next three years further routes to Alicante, Barcelona, Malaga, Palma, Nice and Bergamo were introduced and during the financial year 2012–13 around 4.8 million passengers were carried on some 32,500 flights. By 2014, Jet2 had amassed a fleet of forty-six Boeing jets, including Boeing 757s which were introduced in September 2005. A separate division, Jet2 Holidays, was formed to market inclusive arrangements based around the airline's flights, which served over fifty destinations including Tel Aviv and Sharm el-Sheikh from six UK airports.

EasyJet was the brainchild of Stelios Haji-Ioannou, who had previously been in the family shipping business and had created Stelmar Tankers in 1992 at the age of 25. On 17 March 1995 he launched easyJet with the aid of a $5 million loan from his father. His airline was based at Luton Airport and initially used two leased Boeing 737s to operate low-cost flights from there to Glasgow at fares starting from £29 one way.

Edinburgh was added as a destination on 10 November 1995, and easyJet's first international route, between Luton and Amsterdam, was inaugurated on 24 April 1996. In order to make it easier for passengers to make bookings, the airline's reservations telephone number was emblazoned in large characters along the fuselage of each aircraft, and was duly replaced by the web address when easyJet began selling seats online in April 1998.

A large fleet of Boeing 737s was built up, but in 2002 the airline switched its allegiance to Airbus Industries, announcing a large order for A319 aircraft for delivery from August 2003.

In 2013 easyJet carried over 60 million passengers at a load factor approaching 90 per cent, and by 2014 a fleet of 137 Airbus A319s and A320s was serving 104 destinations.

Ryanair began life in 1985 as a small, conventional scheduled service airline, opening a twice-daily Waterford–Gatwick service with a Bandeirante commuter aircraft in July of that year. It was in the same year that a new Air Service Agreement between the UK and Irish governments opened the door to a second carrier on Dublin–London services, and on 23 May 1986 Ryanair used two leased HS-748 turboprop aircraft to inaugurate budget-fare services between Dublin and Luton airports.

Jet operations followed from 1 December 1986 with a leased One-Eleven aircraft, and by the summer of 1995 Ryanair had become the dominant carrier on the Dublin–London route and had built up a fleet of eleven aircraft, including its first Boeing 737s.

From late 1995, in the new political climate of European airline deregulation, Ryanair began its policy of seeking out small continental airports which were within striking distance of major cities, and persuading them to slash their handling fees and work with Ryanair to generate new services and new markets. On 1 May 1997 the airline opened new routes from Dublin to Charleroi (for Brussels), and Beauvais (for Paris), at fares starting at just £79 one way. From this beginning grew a vast network of low-cost services, and massive orders for new Boeing 737-800 jets. In 2014 Ryanair had a fleet of around 300 aircraft in service on over 1,600 routes throughout Europe.

# Major Aircraft Types Operated by Britain's Holiday Airlines

## AIRBUS INDUSTRIE A320

Advanced technology short/medium-haul jet which pioneered the introduction of 'fly-by-wire' systems in commercial transport aircraft. Powered by two CM56 or V2500 turbofan engines. First single-aisle member of Airbus family of airliners. Accommodation for up to 180 passengers. First entered commercial service with Air France in March 1986. Used for inclusive tour charter flights by Air 2000, Monarch Airlines and Thomas Cook Airlines.

## AIRSPEED AMBASSADOR

Pressurised, medium-haul airliner with high wing and triple tail fins. Powered by two Bristol Centaurus piston engines. Accommodation for up to sixty passengers. Entered commercial service in March 1952 with BEA, who called it their 'Elizabethan' class and used it to relaunch the prestigious 'Silver Wing' lunchtime service to Paris. After retirement from BEA service examples were used for inclusive tour services by Dan-Air, Autair and BKS Air Transport.

## AVIATION TRADERS CARVAIR

Specialised car ferry conversion of Douglas DC-4 carried out by Aviation Traders Engineering to produce larger and longer-range replacement for the Bristol 170 Superfreighters in service with Channel Air Bridge. Retained the four Pratt &

Whitney Twin Wasp piston engines of the DC-4, but new bulbous nose with clamshell loading doors fitted. Could carry up to five cars and twenty-three passengers. Entered service with Channel Air Bridge in March 1962.

## AVRO 748

Short-haul pressurised 'Dakota replacement' design, powered by two Rolls-Royce Dart turboprop engines. Accommodation for up to fifty-eight passengers. Entered service with Skyways Coach-Air on cross-Channel services in spring 1962. Also used by Channel Airways, Autair and BKS Air Transport.

## BAC ONE-ELEVEN

Short/medium-haul jet airliner, designed as successor to Vickers Viscount. Powered by two Rolls-Royce Spey engines mounted at rear of fuselage. Initial srs 200 model entered service with British United Airways on scheduled services in 1965 and later also used on holiday charter flights. Similar srs 300 and 400 models used for inclusive tour flights by British Eagle, Dan-Air, Channel Airways, Autair and Laker Airways. Stretched srs 500 version was designed primarily for inclusive tour market. Used by British United Airways, Caledonian Airways, British Caledonian Airways and Court Line Aviation. Also operated on scheduled services by BEA.

## BOEING 707 AND 720

Long-haul jet airliner used by most of the world's major airlines in the 1960s. Originally entered service on transatlantic flights with Pan American Airways in 1958. Powered by four Pratt & Whitney JT3D or Rolls-Royce Conway turbojet engines. Also served with BOAC, many of whose examples were later acquired by BEA Airtours for inclusive tour work and long-haul charters. Other operators included Dan-Air, British Caledonian, British Eagle and Laker Airways. The Boeing 720B was a lighter and faster development of the 707 and was used by Monarch Airlines.

## BOEING 727

Medium-range jet airliner powered by three Pratt & Whitney engines grouped around the tail. Initially entered service with Eastern Airlines in February 1964.

Over 1,000 of the initial srs 100 model and the stretched srs 200 model sold to airlines worldwide. Accommodation for up to 189 passengers. Dan-Air was first UK operator. Later used by Sabre Airways.

## BOEING 737

Short-haul jet airliner. Along with Douglas DC-9, was a direct competitor to BAC One-Eleven. Powered by two Pratt & Whitney engines. First entered service with Lufthansa in 1968. Sold worldwide, and still in production in 2015. First UK operator was Britannia Airways, which pioneered inclusive tour operations with the type in July 1968. Also used for this purpose by Dan-Air, Air Europe, Monarch Airlines, Orion Airways and British Airtours.

## BOEING 757

Narrow-bodied, single-aisle jet airliner. Powered by two Rolls-Royce or Pratt & Whitney turbofan engines. First entered service in 1983 on scheduled services with Eastern Airlines and British Airways. Used for inclusive tour work by Air Europe, Monarch Airlines, Air 2000 and Britannia Airways.

## BRISTOL 170

Unpressurised high-wing transport aircraft, originally intended for RAF use in Far East during the Second World War, but too late to serve in this role. From 1947 marketed and used successfully as both military and commercial passenger/freight aircraft. Powered by two Bristol Hercules piston engines. Cargo version fitted with clamshell-type nose-loading doors. All-passenger version was named Bristol Wayfarer and could carry up to thirty-two passengers. Used by Silver City Airways to inaugurate cross-Channel car ferry services in July 1948. To meet the high demand for these services the stretched Mk32 Superfreighter, capable of carrying more cars, was developed for Silver City and was also used by Channel Air Bridge.

## BRISTOL BRITANNIA

Pressurised four-engined long-haul airliner, originally built for BOAC Empire routes. Powered by four Bristol Proteus turboprop engines. Original srs 102 version entered service with BOAC in February 1957. After retirement, many examples sold to Britannia Airways and BKS Air Transport and used for inclusive tour work. Stretched srs 300 version was intended for transatlantic scheduled services, but its delayed introduction by BOAC led to its premature retirement and replacement by jets. Srs 300 examples later used by Monarch Airlines to launch inclusive tour services in 1968 and on transatlantic charters by Caledonian Airways.

## CANADAIR ARGONAUT AND NORTH STAR

Long-range development of Douglas DC-4, produced in Canada using Rolls-Royce Merlin piston engines in place of original Pratt & Whitney Twin Wasps. Pressurisation introduced on later examples. Entered service with Trans Canada Airlines as North Star in late 1947 on Montreal–London route. Basically similar version known as Argonaut used by BOAC from August 1949. Accommodation for up to sixty-two passengers. After retirement from mainline service examples of both variants used for inclusive tour work by Overseas Aviation and Derby Airways (later to become British Midland Airways).

## DE HAVILLAND COMET 4/4B/4C

Original Comet 1 was world's first jet airliner in service, but was grounded after series of crashes. Developed Comet 4 operated world's first transatlantic jet service, between London and New York, for BOAC in 1958. Shorter-range Comet 4B used on European services by BEA. Powered by four Rolls-Royce Avon turbojet engines. After retirement from mainline service, large fleet of Comets of all variants used for inclusive tour services by Dan-Air. Comet 4Bs also used for this purpose by BEA Airtours and Channel Airways.

## DOUGLAS C-47 DAKOTA

Short-range unpressurised transport aircraft, mostly powered by two Pratt & Whitney Twin Wasp piston engines. Accommodation for up to thirty-six passengers. Entered service with American Airlines in June 1936 on US coast-to-coast sleeper services. During the Second World War over 13,000 examples produced in USA and Soviet Union. Post-war, thousands acquired by civil operators worldwide, including BEA. Also used as initial equipment for most UK charter airlines, and operated on some of the first inclusive tour services.

# DOUGLAS DC-4

Unpressurised long-range transport aircraft. Design originally sponsored by the major US airlines but production taken over by the US Army Air Force during the Second World War as the C-54 military transport. Powered by four Pratt & Whitney Twin Wasp piston engines. Post-war around 500 aircraft disposed of to airlines and seventy-four new civil examples built. Used on inclusive tour work by Starways, Air Ferry and Invicta Airways. Type also used as basic airframe for Aviation Traders Carvair conversions.

# DOUGLAS DC-7C

Final development of the Douglas DC-4/DC-6/DC-7 line of four-engined transports. Developed to a Pan American Airways' requirement for an airliner capable of flying the Atlantic non-stop in either direction. Powered by four Wright turbo-compound piston engines. Entered service with Pan American in June 1956 and also operated by BOAC. After retirement from mainline service examples used for transatlantic charters by Caledonian Airways from 1961.

# DOUGLAS DC-10

Wide-bodied twin-aisle jet airliner. Direct competitor to Lockheed TriStar. Powered by three General Electric CF-6 turbofan engines, one at base of tailfin and others under wings. Accommodation for up to 380 passengers. Entered service with American Airlines in August 1971. Used by Laker Airways on low-cost Skytrain service to USA and by Monarch Airlines for inclusive tour work.

# HANDLEY PAGE HERMES

Medium-range pressurised airliner powered by four Bristol Hercules piston engines. Accommodation for up to eighty-two passengers. Used by BOAC from August 1950, mainly on African routes. From 1952 began to be disposed of to UK independent airlines. Initially used for trooping flights, but later used on inclusive tour charter flights by Skyways, Silver City Airways, Air Safaris and Falcon Airways.

## LOCKHEED CONSTELLATION

Triple-finned long-range pressurised airliner powered by four Wright Cyclone piston engines. Designed to a Trans World Airlines specification, but initially entered service with Pan American in February 1946. Used by BOAC for transatlantic services. Inaugurated inclusive tour operations for Euravia, and also used by Skyways and Falcon Airways.

## LOCKHEED TRISTAR

Wide-bodied, twin-aisle jet airliner, direct competitor to Douglas DC-10. Powered by three Rolls-Royce RB211 turbofan engines, one at base of tailfin and others on wings. Accommodation for up to 400 passengers. Entered service with Eastern Airlines in April 1972. Used by Court Line Aviation for inclusive tour charters to the Caribbean.

## SHORT SOLENT

Unpressurised flying boat, used by BOAC on scheduled services to Johannesburg in late 1940s. After replacement with BOAC by landplane types, acquired by Aquila Airways and used on routes from Southampton to Madeira and Capri. Powered by two Bristol Hercules piston engines. Accommodation for up to fifty-six passengers on two decks. The last flying boats in airline service, retired at end of September 1950.

## VICKERS VANGUARD

Medium-range pressurised airliner designed as larger successor to Vickers Viscount. Powered by four Rolls-Royce Tyne turboprop engines. Accommodation for up to 139 passengers. Only forty-four built, for service with BEA and Trans Canada Airlines. Several former Trans Canada examples acquired for inclusive tour operations by Invicta Airways.

## VICKERS VIKING

Short-range unpressurised airliner, derived from Wellington bomber design of the Second World War. Used same wings and two Bristol Hercules piston engines, married to new passenger-carrying fuselage. Accommodation for up to thirty-six passengers. Used extensively by BEA on European services from September 1946. After replacement in front-line service, many examples acquired from BEA and other airlines by inclusive tour operators such as Eagle Airways, Air Safaris, Autair and Invicta Airways.

## VICKERS VISCOUNT

Medium-range pressurised airliner, the first turboprop transport to enter airline service. Powered by four Rolls-Royce Dart engines. Entered service with BEA in April 1953 and set new standards of passenger appeal and smoothness of flight. Over 440 built and served worldwide. After retirement from front-line service large numbers used on inclusive tour charters and scheduled services by UK operators such as British United Airways, British Eagle, Starways and Channel Airways.

# Principal Charter Flight Operators to Palma in 1960

| Operator (Nationality) | Passengers Carried to/from Palma During Year |
|---|---|
| Transair Sweden (Sweden) | 23,000 |
| Overseas Aviation (UK) | 22,000 |
| Flying Enterprise (Denmark) | 18,000 |
| British United Airways (UK) | 17,000 |
| Balair (Switzerland) | 16,000 |
| Condor (West Germany) | 14,000 |
| Deutsche Flugdienst (West Germany) | 10,000 |
| Tradair (UK) | 9,000 |
| Continentale (West Germany) | 9,000 |
| LTU (West Germany) | 9,000 |
| Cunard Eagle Airways (UK) | 8,000 |
| BKS Air Transport (UK) | 6,000 |
| Starways (UK) | 6,000 |
| Airnautic (France) | 5,000 |

# UK CHARTER AIRLINE NAMES TO DISAPPEAR DURING 1989–98

| | | |
|---|---|---|
| 1989 | Paramount Airways | Ceased operations. |
| 1989 | Cal Air International | Sold to British Airways and renamed Novair. |
| 1989 | Orion Airways | Merged into Britannia Airways. |
| 1990 | British Island Airways | Ceased operations. |
| 1990 | Novair International | Ceased operations. |
| 1991 | Air Europe | Ceased operations. |
| 1991 | TEA UK | Ceased operations. |
| 1992 | Dan-Air | Acquired by British Airways. |
| 1993 | Inter European Airways | Merged into Airtours International. |
| 1994 | Ambassador Airways | Ceased operations. |
| 1995 | Caledonian Airways | Sold by British Airways to Inspirations Group. |
| 1996 | Excalibur Airways | Ceased operations. |
| 1998 | Leisure International Airways | Merged into Air 2000. |
| 1998 | Flying Colours Airlines | Merged into Airworld. |

# TOUR OPERATOR/CHARTER AIRLINE ALLIANCES

## TOUR OPERATOR/CHARTER AIRLINE ALLIANCES AS AT JUNE 1987:

| Tour Operator | Charter Airline |
| --- | --- |
| Clarksons Holidays | Court Line Aviation |
| International Leisure Group (Intasun, Global, Club 18–30 etc.) | Air Europe |
| Horizon Travel Group (Horizon Holidays, Broadway, Holiday Club etc.) | Orion Airways |
| British Airways Holidays Group (Flair, Enterprise, Martin Rooks, Sovereign Holidays etc.) | British Airtours |
| Globus Gateway Group (Cosmos Holidays etc.) | Monarch Airlines |
| Rank Organisation (Wings, OSL, Blue Sky Holidays etc.) | Cal Air International (50 per cent share with BCAL) |

## TOUR OPERATOR/CHARTER AIRLINE ALLIANCES AS AT AUGUST 1998:

| Tour Operator | Charter Airline |
| --- | --- |
| Thomson Group | Britannia Airways |
| Airtours Group | Airtours International |
| Cosmos Group | Monarch Airlines |
| First Choice Group | Air 2000/Leisure International |
| Inspirations Group | Caledonian Airways/Peach Air |
| Thomas Cook/Sunworld Group | Airworld/Flying Colours |

# UK CHARTER AIRLINES FLEETS AND TOTAL SEAT CAPACITY BY TYPE

## AS AT SUMMER 1994:

| | |
|---|---|
| Air 2000 | 15 Boeing 757 200s (total 3,495 seats) and 4 Airbus A320s (total 720 seats). |
| Airtours International | 2 Boeing 767-300s (total 652 seats) and 2 Boeing 757-200s (total 466 seats) plus 2 Airbus A320-200s (total 360 seats) and 8 MD-83s (total 1,336 seats). |
| Air UK Leisure | 6 Boeing 737-400s (total 1,032 seats). |
| Ambassador Airways | 2 Boeing 757-200s (total 466 seats). |
| Britannia Airways | 10 Boeing 767-200s (total 2,900 seats) and 12 Boeing 757-200s (total 2,820 seats). |
| British World Airlines | 3 BAC One-Eleven srs 500s (total 357 seats) and 2 BAe 146-300s (total 220 seats). |
| Caledonian Airways | 1 DC-10-30 (356 seats), 6 Boeing 757-200s (total 1,398 seats) and 5 TriStar (total 1,965 seats). |
| European Aviation Aircharter | 3 BAC One-Eleven srs 500s (total 312 seats). |
| Excalibur Airways | 4 Airbus A320-200s (total 720 seats). |
| Monarch Airlines | 4 Airbus A300-600s (total 1,444 seats), 8 Boeing 757-200s (total 1,880 seats), 7 Airbus A320-200s (total 1,260 seats) and 1 Boeing 737-300 (148 seats). |
| Palmair Flightline | 1 BAe 146-300 (110 seats). |
| Total seats on market | 25,069. |

# SOURCES

## BOOKS AND MAGAZINES

Belcher, Robert, *Blackbushe* (GMS Enterprises, 2009).
Bray, Robert, and Vladimir Raitz, *Flight to the Sun* (Continuum, 2001).
Cuthbert, Geoffrey, *Flying to the Sun* (Hodder & Stoughton, 1987).
Dagwell, Keith J., *Silver City Airways – Pioneers of the Skies* (The History Press, 2010).
Halford-MacLeod, Guy, *Britain's Airlines*, Vols 1 & 2 (Tempus Publishing, 2006 and 2007).
Hedges, David, *The Eagle Years* (TAHS, 2001).
Merton Jones, A.C., *British Independent Airlines Since 1946* (LAAS and MAS, 1976).
*Propliner* magazine (various).
Simons, Graham M., *Airfield Focus – Luton* (GMS Enterprises, 2008).
Simons, Graham M., *Gatwick – From a Flying Club to a Major Hub* (GMS Enterprises, 2010).
Simons, Graham M., *The Spirit of Dan-Air* (GMS Enterprises, 1993).
Thaxter, David, *The History of British Caledonian Airways 1928–1988* (Golden Lion Foundation, 2011).
Vomhof, Klaus, *Leisure Airlines of Europe* (Scoval Publishing, 2001).
Wickstead, Maurice J., *Airlines of the British Isles Since 1919* (DVD) (Air-Britain, 2014).

## WEBSITES AND ONLINE FORUMS

British Caledonian – A tribute website (www.british-caledonian.com)
British Eagle website (www.britisheagle.net)
Farnborough Aviation Group – 'Blackbushe Pics from the Past' forum (forum.keypublishing.com)

Flightglobal Archive website (www.flightglobal.com/pdfarchive/)
Gatwick Aviation Society website (www.gatwickaviationsociety.org.uk)
'Homage to Court Line' forum (groups.yahoo.com)
Silver City Association website (www.silvercityairways.com)
Skyways Coach-Air website (www.skylineaviation.co.uk/skyways.htm)